AF174068

Self-Knowledge

Sci-Knowledge

Self-Knowledge

BEGINNING PHILOSOPHY RIGHT HERE AND NOW

Stephen Hetherington

BROADVIEWGUIDES to PHILOSOPHY

For Parveen,
Her self

Speak of me as I am. Nothing extenuate,
Nor set down aught in malice.
> Othello, in Shakespeare's *Othello*

Each mortal thing does one thing and the same:
Deals out that being indoors each one dwells;[1]
Selves—goes itself; *myself* it speaks and spells,
Crying *What I do is me: for that I came*.
> Gerard Manley Hopkins, "Inversnaid"

And you, Helen, what should I give you?
...
I would give you back yourself,
And power to discriminate
What you want and want it not too late
> Edward Thomas, "And You, Helen"

---

[1] Manifests that way of existing, with which it must live.

© 2007 Stephen Hetherington

All rights reserved. The use of any part of this publication reproduced, transmitted in any form or by any means, electronic, mechanical, photocopying, recording, or otherwise, or stored in a retrieval system, without prior written consent of the publisher—or in the case of photocopying, a licence from Access Copyright (Canadian Copyright Licensing Agency), One Yonge Street, Suite 1900, Toronto, Ontario M5E 1E5—is an infringement of the copyright law.

Library and Archives Canada Cataloguing in Publication

Hetherington, Stephen Cade
    Self-knowledge : beginning philosophy right here and now / Stephen Hetherington.

(Broadview guides to philosophy)
Includes bibliographical references.
ISBN 978-1-55111-798-0

    1. Self (Philosophy). 2. Self-knowledge, Theory of. I. Title. II. Series.

BD438.5.H48 2007   126   C2007-900786-4

Broadview Press is an independent, international publishing house, incorporated in 1985. Broadview believes in shared ownership, both with its employees and with the general public; since the year 2000 Broadview shares have traded publicly on the Toronto Venture Exchange under the symbol BDP.

We welcome comments and suggestions regarding any aspect of our publications—please feel free to contact us at the addresses below or at broadview@broadviewpress.com.

North America
PO Box 1243, Peterborough, Ontario, Canada K9J 7H5
PO Box 1015, 3576 California Road, Orchard Park, NY, USA 14127
Tel: (705) 743-8990; Fax: (705) 743-8353
email: customerservice@broadviewpress.com

UK, Ireland, and continental Europe
NBN International, Estover Road, Plymouth, UK PL6 7PY
Tel: 44 (0) 1752 202300; Fax: 44 (0) 1752 202330
Email: enquiries@nbninternational.com

Australia and New Zealand
UNIREPS, University of New South Wales
Sydney, NSW, Australia 2052
Tel: 61 2 9664 0999; Fax: 61 2 9664 5420
email: info.press@unsw.edu.au

www.broadviewpress.com

This book is printed on paper containing 100% post-consumer fibre.

Broadview Press acknowledges the financial support of the Government of Canada through the Book Publishing Industry Development Program (BPIDP) for our publishing activities.

Typesetting by Aldo Fierro.

PRINTED IN CANADA

CONTENTS

Day 3   What Kind of Thing Would Self-Knowledge Be?

Day 4

How Might Self-Knowledge Be Gained?

Day 5

Confronting Doubts about Whether
Self-Knowledge is Possible

ACKNOWLEDGEMENTS

Stephen Buckle, Scott Campbell, Adam Dickerson, Robert Gray, Adam Morton, Parveen Seehra, and Robert Young provided splendid advice on stylistic, philosophical, and organisational details. Three anonymous referees also helped greatly, critically encouraging and orientating the project.

WHY?

"This philosophy—do you say that it lies behind everything?"
"Yes, I think so. It tries to discover what is good and true."
"Then, my boy, you had better read as much of it as you can."
E.M. Forster, *The Longest Journey*

How would you describe yourself? Try listing some of your more significant features. Now ask, "Why do I think of myself in *those* terms, in *those* ways?" Most likely, you've adopted concepts, values, and patterns of reasoning from other people—parents, friends, teachers, advertisers, journalists, and so on. Subtly, they could have set in place many aspects of how you think of yourself; and is that *good*? If they're completely correct about you, maybe so; but *are* they? Possibly not. Have you taken this possibility seriously? Or have you uncritically fallen into thinking about yourself much as others do? Is it time for *you* to work out, for yourself, what you're really like?

Imagine reflecting, shortly before your death, upon your life as a whole. Suppose you find yourself thinking in this way: "I never *tested* what others said about me. I never fully *chose* how to think about myself. Instead, I did what was easiest—thinking like everyone else, without properly scrutinizing alternatives." That sounds like a potentially sad moment.

So, how about taking some control now? Seize the opportunity; don't delay. Otherwise, a worrying question arises. Might you *have* less of a self to know in the first place, if you aren't thinking *for* yourself about yourself? Might you *be* less of a self—merely a composite of, or conduit for, other people's opinions, say?

Those questions suddenly struck me about myself, one day last summer. Disconcerted, I began thinking about little else. For five intense days, that's what I did. First I tried to clear my mind, emptying it of needless assumptions. I sought mental freshness. My goal was to reflect upon myself as if, at least at the outset, I didn't know myself *at all*.

Why? I wanted to come to know myself *anew*—"from scratch," not automatically accepting what others would say, and what I had previously taken for granted, about me. Could I do that? Was it realistically possible for me to question lots of everyday beliefs about myself—about my body, thoughts, character, history, and future? Would this just be silly? Or might it reveal exciting new possibilities—fresh concepts and ways of thinking—for genuine self-understanding? I hoped to find out.

It felt satisfying, too, trying to take such *personal responsibility* for my sense of myself. It was like an initiation rite, a step towards "growing up" and maturing. I was thinking *for* myself, *by* myself. Would I thereby become *more* of a self?

This wasn't always emotionally easy, as you'll see. Unusual ways of thinking arose, testing my mental composure and resilience. Still, that's what it is like to risk leaving behind a familiar self-conception: "nothing ventured, nothing gained." I've honestly tried to know some fundamental aspects of myself, opening my mind to the idea that, previously, I hadn't known myself as well as I'd assumed I did.

These meditations are the result. I hope you find in them a worthwhile and helpful example of how one might seek such personal development and self-understanding. Knowing oneself is part of being intelligent about oneself, I suspect; who *wouldn't* rather be like that?

LEARNING WITH THIS BOOK

You can help yourself by approaching these resulting meditations with an eye upon how to learn from them. Here are some hints.

The book is composed of many sections. To almost every one of them (the few exceptions being clarificatory or "bridging" sections), I might have appended this question: Is that section *right* in what it's saying about people? Any careful reader would need to answer that key question—if truth is our primary philosophical goal; which it is.

Whenever you are trying to answer that main question, of course, other ones will arise. What was the section's main suggestion or hypothesis? What conclusion was reached? What reasons or pieces of evidence were used? (Are there sub-arguments for sub-conclusions—functioning also as evidence for the section's main conclusion?) Is the section's conclusion true? Is all of the suggested evidence true? How well does the evidence support the conclusion?

I should mention that some pieces of reasoning are presented via questioning or (more often) via a mixture of intersecting questions and proposals. A sequence of questions can be an inquiring or non-dogmatic way of developing a line of thought. A back-and-forth of questions and proposals can be a non-dogmatic way of formulating and testing ideas.

In such ways, then, the book is full of ideas and lines of thought with which readers might well disagree. Go ahead; do so. Say why, though; and that's how constructive philosophical thinking and discussion will begin.

Oh, and don't forget to ponder those questions that appear between sections and at the end of each chapter. They're not trivial "review" questions. They're philosophically expansive, sometimes not *directly* about what has been said in the preceding section. They raise related thoughts and quirky possibilities—which is how a lot of serious philosophical thinking develops, as one remains open to surprise and experiment, all the while pursuing new ideas. Try answering those questions; you don't know in advance where this will lead. The fact that many of the questions are *fun* will be a welcome bonus.

KNOWING ONE'S PHYSICAL NATURE

> You know you've got the brain of a four-year old child, and I bet he
> was glad to get rid of it.
>
> Groucho Marx, in the movie *Horse Feathers*

1.1 "I've just gotta be me"

Often, we make vague and conflicting claims about ourselves and
others. Do we really understand ourselves? Here's one reason why I
ask that question.

I've frequently heard people being told that they're unique and wonderful: "You are what you are. That makes you special, one of a kind. It
also makes you important and valuable. Your uniqueness is precious.
Don't ever change. Be true to yourself." Many people find no difficulty
in thinking of themselves in that way! The sentiment charms them.

On the other hand, I've often listened to people being exhorted to
"be all they can be." ("You can be anything. Just choose!") Motivational speakers become rich on such stirring stuff. Unsurprisingly, people
love hearing it. So much is promised.

When combined, though, those two ways of talking confuse me.
Am I special and thereby worthwhile, even terrific? Yet must I try to be
different, so as to improve, becoming even better? Which is it to be? Is

this Me good enough? Or is a better one needed? Already, I'm unsure how to think of myself. Each way of thinking sounds uplifting; yet they seem to clash with each other. I don't want simply to believe everything that pleases me, making me feel good about myself. I want *truth*, as what ultimately cannot be escaped.

Maybe I can make those conflicting ways of talking less confusing. Initially, I'll try applying them to my body, my physical self, in particular. (This is because it's so tangible, so real, to me and others.) Here goes.

Is my body so worthy of respect and admiration, so significant? Well, it's the only one I have! It is special, in the sense of being unique—located here, nowhere else, right now, distinct from other bodies. However, that isn't enough to make it especially noteworthy or good. So, should I try to make *it* all that it can be? That sounds excellent. Yet to the extent that my body can be improved, is it not already so good? Especially so, given how *many* ways there seem to be of improving it. The following thinking occurs to me:

> To the extent that this body can be improved, it's flawed. This makes it that much less worthy of admiration. Each new improvement would reveal, retrospectively, an inadequacy in the body (which had been able to be improved in that way). This body would be seen, with each new improvement, to have previously been less and less admirable, considered *as* a body.

What is completely admirable shouldn't need improvement. Even what is fairly admirable should need little improvement. Again, therefore, I find myself confronting the thought that this body I call "mine" is *not* so admirable—even less so, to the extent that it can be improved. To that extent (and people are routinely exhorted to seek such personal improvement), it isn't such a fine specimen after all. Blast!

Now I should combine that thought with this question: How much can this body be improved anyway? If it cannot be improved much, or even at all, perhaps it is condemned to remaining not-so-admirable, perhaps much less good than is possible for a body. The following reasoning also occurs to me:

> To improve my body would be to alter it. However, does altering it a great deal risk making it less and less *my* body? If so, there's a chance that it's *impossible* to improve my body very much—so that it continues *being* my own body. (Is this a pleasing idea, because my body cannot be improved greatly? Or is it depressing, for the same reason?)

This is difficult reasoning to assess. Here's a way of making it easier to grasp.

I might decide that I could improve my body through increased exercise, improved nutrition, and body-bending yoga. Would strength training help, too? Should I then reach for steroids? Or human growth hormones? Would it be a good idea to contemplate cosmetic surgery? Are these ways of improving this body? Such questions make me uneasy. One reason is that I'm unsure whether the resulting person would really be me. My present body would have been "traded in" for a new one. Perhaps *I* would thereby have become new. People talk casually of "a new me"; possibly, there would *actually* be "a new me." But if so, such "improvement" could be interpreted as a subtle form of death (yes, death) for my present body! Right now, that idea is personally weighty, as I decide whether to undergo such improvement. Should I welcome it? Should I shun it? As I consider the question at this present moment, I don't want this present body to die.

I don't immediately know the answers to those questions. Like anyone else, I take much for granted, even about myself. I have preconceptions, opinions, beliefs, views, and thoughts—some of them about what I take to be my physical self. Yet possibly they aren't *knowledge* of my physical self. (Although I think they are, maybe this thought—about those other thoughts—is itself not knowledge.) Perhaps they are *just* preconceptions, opinions, beliefs, views, and thoughts.

Real knowledge is what I want. Indeed, I want some highly signifi-cant self-knowledge, because my question is whether I really know my own body. That could sound absurd ("How could I *not* have that knowl-edge?"), except that there *is* a chance of my lacking that knowledge. It isn't that I would experience a total lack of information on the matter. The problem is more subtle. Specifically, maybe I lack the knowledge of what my own body is, if I don't know what actual or imagined *changes* a body could undergo before ceasing to be mine. If I don't know every possible circumstance in which some particular body (such as a sur-gically enhanced one, including one that has had organ transplants) would *not* be mine, potentially I cannot know, at least not always, when a particular body *is* mine. So, I mightn't always know whether a particular body *is* mine. (Presumably, there are limits to what changes this present body could incur before it would cease being mine. Or are there none?)

It's bewildering to contemplate that idea of not knowing which body is mine. "It's this one. Over here: this one," I say—as you would expect me to do. Yet what, exactly, *is* "this"? I point at a body, right here, right now. (*This* finger points at *this* stomach.) However, that act of pointing isn't enough to answer the more subtle question of what changes the body being pointed at could undergo before it would cease being mine. At best, the pointing gives me a superficial knowledge of my body. Can I gain deeper knowledge of it?

I'll begin optimistically. This might appear to be the *easiest* sort of self-knowledge to gain. ("Just be aware of one's body. That's all it takes—simple!") But even that knowledge needn't be readily avail-able. I'll seek it by "starting afresh" in how I think about what my body is. I will therefore be questioning much I've always taken for granted. That's difficult to do, because I must begin thinking about myself quite differently from how I usually do. I must remember, though, that my usual views about myself might be very superficial, and that I'll be trying to know myself more deeply. It will be as if I'm having an "out of body" experience, reflecting on my body in a way that's new for me, wondering about it in a "detached" way. But if I don't attempt to move much beyond what I currently assume about myself (even if this involves posing uncomfortable questions), I'll never really test my present self-image. I'll merely continue embracing whatever I already accept about what I assume is myself; and it's possible that, until now, I've never thought particularly well about such matters. I must try harder.

Yet is there a danger even in this? Yes! For I would be trying to do to my mind what I've already described as not necessarily possible for my body. That is, I would be trying to be all that I *can* be as a thinker about myself. Does this suggest that my present view of myself can be improved—that it is not so admirable, certainly not perfect? Maybe. Does that present view of myself need to change, by becoming all that *it* can be? If so, the following awkward question arises. If my current self-image were to change deeply, mightn't my present mind change, in effect departing—being replaced by what I would hope is a new and better one? (Little changes to my self-image might not matter; but I'm wondering about large ones.) Such mental improvement could then amount to the *death* of my present mind—"death by improvement"!

The decision about whether to run that risk is therefore profound, more so than casual reflection would have revealed. I'm now hesitant, again. My present mind is feeling some fear at the idea of departing—of being replaced by an improved mind. Maybe such a fear is part of why people often shy away from new and challenging thoughts.

Simple question. What is the simplest substantial question people could ever ask about themselves?

1.2   My left hand

I will begin cautiously, then, when seeking to know my physical nature. Do I even have one? Seemingly yes, because I seem to have a body. There is a body here; is it mine? Maybe it even *is* me, all there is of me. Is that possible?

Let me see. What do I know about this body? Do I know that it is mine?

I'm holding up a hand, a left hand, while writing this. How do I know that it's my own hand? I see a hand; but do I see its "mine-ness"? This isn't clear. There's nothing in the hand itself—is there?—that says "I belong to S.H." (My name isn't written or tattooed on it! But even if it were, how would I know that it's *my* name? And even if I did, how could I be sure that it wasn't my name put on a hand that wasn't mine?) I *treat* it as being mine. Why, though? Surely, or so I feel, there's no other way in which I could sensibly treat it. Is this emotional on my part? Or is it more purely rational? I don't want to become emotionally "detached" or "alienated" from my own body; and this is the closest complete body I ever see. Equally, I don't wish to become emotionally "attached" to some hand that isn't really my own. That would be unhealthy. So again, how (if at all) do I know that this hand is mine?

Here's a thought:

> Maybe the mine-ness of the hand I'm inspecting is its history, its having a past. The hand has done this and that; it's been here and there—always helping me, accompanying me.

But as I look at the hand right now, that history itself isn't something I observe. Do I see the hand's past? (People often make claims like, "I can see his life's history in his face.") No, I don't believe so. All I see is the hand now, as it is now—not its history, what it has been. (To that, though, I might reply, "That isn't a problem. I use my memory, not just current observations." That's a natural suggestion. Nonetheless, might even memory not give me the knowledge I want? I'll try to remember to return to this thought in a little while.)

I've become accustomed to taking for granted the mine-ness of that hand, when seeing it so repeatedly, so unthinkingly, so often, so nearby.

Even so, I'll try to imagine waking up from sleep, feeling nothing, blinking—only to observe this hand by itself, apparently floating in front of me, detached from any body, shining brightly in the darkness. Would I think, "Oh, there's my hand"? Perhaps not. The question is whether I would know it instantly and visually as mine; and I'm not sure that I would.

This isn't to say I *couldn't* know a hand as being mine (although I'm yet to prove that I do have this knowledge). As it happens, I don't regard my hand as particularly distinctive in appearance. What if it was, though? It could have a distracting birthmark; there might have been a unique tattoo; an unusual shape is possible. "I'd know my hand anywhere," I would proclaim, "Only it—nothing else—has this pattern on it." As well it might; but is that what's needed if I'm to know my own hand? Hopefully, no—because if such distinguishing features are needed for a hand to be known as the particular hand it is, then I *don't* know my own hand. (In this respect, I suspect, I'm like most people.)

Someone might attempt to reassure me along these lines:

> Surely you know it "from within." You know that it is your body because, within limits, you can *control* it (and no one else can control it as you do). You could decide to move your fingers—and then notice them moving.

Yet that correlation might be a coincidence. I would not know *surely* that I was controlling all of the hand's actions. I'm not totally convinced that I can observe the actual something-within-me-making-the-fingers-move. When I try to do so ... right now ... of what am I conscious? Perhaps I know that I'm deciding to move the fingers, and that they then move. Or maybe I look at them, seeing them start to move, before *inferring* that I must have decided to move them. It feels more like the latter than the former; but if I don't yet know that the fingers are mine in the first place, I'm not well-placed to know that there's a decision by me behind the moving-of-them. That is, I wouldn't know that it's me controlling them, by knowing first that they're mine and that *therefore* my decision is controlling them. (Maybe it depends upon whether I know that there is a Me *apart* from the body. I won't think about that today—maybe tomorrow.)

All of this thinking is rendered more puzzling by the fact that I see, day after day, what I believe is my left hand. I see it as often as I see anything in the world, more frequently than almost any other part of me. Possibly, there's no bodily part that we notice more often than our hands. This makes it even more remarkable that there's a real question as to whether I would know my left hand if I were to encounter it in the unusual circumstances I described a moment ago. Even though I believe my hand to be a crucial piece of me, one I see repeatedly—and even though I describe it as something in its own right, something I "have" (as I have a favourite possession?)—I mightn't recognise it if I were to see it on its own, isolated, visually detached from the rest of me. What does this show about my awareness of my own body? I'm left unconfident that I know it thoroughly or completely. There could be limits to what my eyes, for instance, tell me about my body—even when they *seem* helpful.

> *Expressive question.* Why do we say that fingers, in particular, can express someone's personality? Which other parts of a body do so? Which ones don't?

1.3   Other body parts

That problem of bodily self-knowledge, as it could be called, runs deeper still as a challenge confronting my attempt to know myself. It isn't simply about knowing my own left hand. The same kind of worry applies to other parts of my body, maybe all parts of it. My left hand is merely one among many possible examples. What of my left foot, say?

I'll imagine just a left foot's being illuminated in the surrounding darkness, so that, upon waking one morning, startled, first meeting the image, I don't see the rest of me, not even my left leg. My own left foot is hardly so eye-catchingly distinctive as to be recognisable as mine—yes, mine! mine!—in that circumstance. I wouldn't know it as mine simply by gazing upon it in the dark, with nothing telling me that the foot I'm perusing is my own. No one else would know it as mine simply by looking at it, either. Yet in practice I do usually think that my eyes would be enough to let me know this left foot as my own. Looking downwards, I remove a shoe; and there it is—a foot, *my* foot. Still, is it only *extrinsically* mine? (What does that mean? When I am using a packet of vitamins or aspirin or whatever, there's an important relationship between me and that packet. Once I empty the packet, however, that relationship ends. I discard the packet. It becomes merely another object with no continuing link to me, no longer significant for me. A new packet, a full one, replaces it in that respect. Is my use of the left foot that I see before me—right now, down there—like my use of a packet of supportive vitamins? If that left foot were to be replaced by another, would I no longer care about the previous one—even though I care greatly about it at the moment?)

That question is difficult enough; and now the challenge of understanding my relationship to this body is about to become even more challenging. Perhaps all possible *combinations* of body parts are also vulnerable to the kind of thinking I've been developing.

Again I look down, this time noticing a left shin *plus* a left foot—and believing that this is a more complex part of myself. How do I know it is, though? Does that shin-plus-foot look like it's mine? Yes, it does; then again, no, it does not. What do I mean by this indecisiveness? In itself, the shin-plus-foot doesn't look as though it is mine, because it doesn't look like *any* particular person's. It has no special marks. (Imagine my finding a photo of it, with no explanatory caption attached. I wouldn't exclaim, "Aha! That's mine!") But in another way, it does look like it's mine, simply by being attached to a body that's mine.

Or so I say. It's what I'm used to thinking. How helpful is it, though? It reflects how people routinely talk about their own body parts. ("That foot is mine because it's part of my body. This hand is mine, for the same reason.") Nevertheless, the same ownership questions arise about the *rest* of the body, too. So, I cannot merely assume that, because I know it—the body as a whole—as mine, I *therefore* know a particular part of it (such as this foot or that hand) as mine.

For instance, someone might suggest that I see the hand's being mine, because I see that it's part of my body. However, this way of talking would assume my knowing already—in some independent way—which body is mine. (If I was to try supporting that assumption, I might reason like this: "Here's my body as a whole. Hence, here's my hand. It is *a* hand—which I may conclude is *my* hand, because I see that it is part of my *body*.") The assumption would be that I possess some other assured or conclusive way of knowing which body is mine—so that then I can know, by looking, that this hand or that foot is also mine (simply by being part of that body which was already known to be mine). Yet is that assumption true?

I ask this, because it *isn't* obvious that I have another way of knowing which body is mine; and if I don't, what follows? This problematic question would remain: If there's no part of me (such as a left hand or foot) that I know in itself to be mine, how do I know that the whole body—which is composed of those parts—is mine? In other words, which would I know first—the body as a whole, or its parts? And again, *how* would I know whichever of these I know first? By sight? That would be convenient. I don't believe it's so simple, though.

I'm told that the body as a whole and its parts share a DNA code. However, maybe that's too complicated a fact to help me right now. As I sit here, using my eyes, I don't assess a particular left hand as being mine because of its DNA. I make that assessment, based on ... what? Convenience? Habit? At this very moment, I'm unsure. Moreover, even if I know that a DNA code is being shared, this doesn't tell me what makes a particular code *mine*. If I don't already know which body parts are mine, I cannot know that the DNA *from* some particular body part is mine.

Could that problem be avoided by an identifying microchip, say, being inserted within me? Would this be the only way to know myself authoritatively? The idea is that I could identify a body as mine, only once someone else—some "official," an authority—has done so (perhaps before placing the personalized microchip under my skin). There's something disturbing (even if intriguing) in the thought that I could know about myself only through someone else's doing so.

> *Bodily question.* Is the ability to experience bodily pain or discomfort essential to knowing one's body?

1.4   Hidden body parts

Even if I could know a hand or foot as mine, to what *extent* would I thereby know myself? Thankfully, there's more to me than a hand and a foot. Yet won't I have only a lesser kind of knowledge (if any at all) of many of my other parts? Maybe there's something memorable for me about the appearance of my right hand, for example, but that isn't true of the back of my head, my back itself, the bottom of my foot, my heels, the backs of my legs, my internal organs, and ... oh, so many body parts. Nor *should* they be familiar to me; how narcissistic (and what a contortionist, perhaps with X-ray vision) I would be, if they were!

I assume they're present, playing vital structural roles in my body; I wish them well; I rarely sense them, though. (I spend little time looking at them, smelling them, or touching them. I can't "direct" my mind upon them, feeling their "internal extension" or whatever it's called.) They may as well be hidden from me, because I wouldn't recognise them visually if I were shown photographs of them by themselves. Accordingly, I must concede, there are aspects of this body which I take for granted but which, possibly, I don't know as mine. I'm almost never both able and motivated to observe them myself, at least for long. I don't have images of them preserved within my mind. I'm not sure what they are like.

Not-quite-hidden question. What is the most revealing question that could ever be asked about a person? Could some languages be better equipped than others to ask such a question?

1.5   A methodological moment: being philosophical

So far, I've been entertaining some surprising and puzzling thoughts, ones that "normal living" only infrequently prompts or encourages. Where do they come from? What is their point?

They are philosophical, it seems. They arise because I'm trying to think for myself, about myself (so far, about my body). I'm not consulting official authorities (who would they be?) or science (it doesn't ask these questions). I'm seeking clarity and precision—more so than normal. Already, I'm trying to remove some confusion from how I might ordinarily think about myself. *Can* I do this? It's not so difficult to begin being philosophical; but can I stay with it, not stopping too soon?

Hmm. That, I don't yet know. I'll find out only as I proceed. I want to know myself philosophically—deeply, significantly, insightfully. But that's not all: I would like this to be part of coming to think more philosophically about—and even to know—the world in general, or at least the world with which I interact. Let's see whether that's possible.

Completeness question. Is it important to know everything about oneself? How does one know in advance which, if any, aspects of oneself needn't be known?

1.6   Mirrors

Now back to the problem of bodily self-knowledge. Are there limits to that sort of questioning? How do I know that a certain whole body—this one—is mine?

I can imagine looking across a room at an entire body, one that's standing, moving a little, hesitating, stopping. I ask myself, "Who is that ordinary-looking person?" Suppose it's me. Then I would have to know it's me. Right? Wrong! I mightn't recognise myself. There are several ways for this to occur. I mightn't have realized that I was looking at myself in a large mirror. Or perhaps I was seeing a hologram of myself. I could even have been gazing upon—while being deceived by—a visual recording of myself, being shown on a hidden screen. It was me, and I didn't realize this. (The person whom I saw wasn't moving as I was while watching.) I was seeing what was actually my body, without knowing that I was doing so.

Is this possible? I think so. Near the end of my time at high school (in my mathematics class), I shared a desk with someone whom I was so—*so*—close to convincing that I didn't know what I looked like. I *almost* had him believing that I had never seen myself. "We have no mirrors in my house," I said, "I have no idea what my face looks like." "Yes?" he asked, "Really? Gosh." Then he hesitated, before conceding, "Wow." He hesitated again. I renewed the explanation. He was impressed, before hesitating once more. He could not *quite* believe me. He all-but did, though. It wasn't because he was unintelligent, either. In a way, he was being more intelligent than many people. He was opening his mind to a real, even if unusual, possibility. (That's far from stupid. The overly easy way of using one's mind is to consider only usual possibilities, having only standard thoughts.) I could have grown up in a house without mirrors. I might never have noticed my reflection in a shop window. It was possible for me never to have seen myself in a mirror at a friend's house. I need never have realized that these were available ways of observing one's appearance. So, I needn't have known that it was possible for me to find out what I looked like.

Still, in fact I did use those ways of gaining a mental picture of what I took to be myself. Hence, is there no problem about my knowing what my body looks like? Unfortunately, even this isn't completely clear—because there is a residual worry, easily overlooked. It is the fact that

I *had* to use those mirrors if I was to gain such knowledge. I depended on them for knowing what I looked like. Yet did I ever check the accuracy of those mirrors? No. I assumed they were normal, accurate; and although that assumption is conventional, this doesn't guarantee its being true. Maybe the mirrors weren't accurate. This is possible.

The worry runs deeper still. How *could* I have known those mirrors were accurate? Do I have independent ways of checking on a mirror's accuracy? I could use another mirror. But that provides no guarantee. It's possible for all the mirrors I've used to have been inaccurate. Maybe all have been distorting, making me look different to how I really am. Of course, a cheering possibility is raised by that thought: perhaps I'm better-looking in reality than I've always seemed to be to myself—all of those mirrors having distorted my appearance in an unflattering way. Wait a moment, though. If that possibility exists, this not-so-cheering possibility is no less available: all of those mirrors could have been *flattering* distorters. I might be worse-looking than I've thought I am. Oh well.

Accordingly, the worry isn't just that I might have had the bad luck to use only "trick" mirrors. The more disturbing possibility is that maybe all mirrors distort. They needn't do this in a weird way, making us suspicious as soon as we use them. But they could still mislead, even subtly, never causing us to think they're playing tricks. I wouldn't have noticed this happening; nor would I have noticed its not happening. And if I cannot ever have known of its not happening, perhaps I've never really known that I was seeing my face as it actually is. Indeed, I mightn't have known that I was seeing my body as it actually is. What shape do I have? I could unwittingly deceive myself. How do I look to others? Do I look to myself as I *should* look, to a perfect observer? Do I really know? Should I suspend judgement? (Yet it isn't clear to me that I'm genuinely able—psychologically able, emotionally able—to suspend judgement about such matters. I'm unsure whether I could live a full life with no mental representation of how I look. My life would be dramatically different if I literally lacked, any self-image! People *have* lived like that. For instance, not until the Italian Renaissance were self-portraits first painted, with apparently perfect clear glass mirrors first appearing only then. Still, because I do possess a visual self-image, the thought of losing it, and of not replacing it with any new one, feels disorienting.)

Wait a moment. Before I become too startled by these ideas, perhaps there is a way of checking on whether mirrors are distorting. I look at someone other than myself; I look at his or her reflection in a mirror; and I notice whether that reflection is accurate. If it is, presumably this mirror is just as accurate in portraying me.

However, even this needn't be straightforward, because that reflection of myself has to be *used* accurately by me, if it's to give me knowledge. Maybe I interpret or react to it inaccurately. Nor do people always see others accurately. Indeed, they don't always see themselves accurately. If I have an eating disorder, for example, my body can be quite different to how it appears to my eyes, whenever I use a mirror. And what of short-sightedness, or even simple vanity? There are psychological failings, too. Many men (I've heard) tend to see themselves, in mirrors, as being in better physical condition and form than is accurate! Many women (I've also heard) tend, sometimes tragically, to make the opposite mistake about themselves.

Reflective question. In what ways, if any, is it good to know what one looks like?

1.7   My skin

Now I'm becoming a little worried. How much can observation tell me about my body anyway, even when I'm not relying on mirrors and the like?

When looking at what I think is my skin, for example, I generally see a mainly pale expanse. It is, I would say, an unremarkable mixture of pink and white and brown. Do I really know it's like that, though? Are those colours part of this skin as it is in itself? I'm not sure. I've been told that what I see in a coloured surface is partly a matter of how my eyes are processing light signals they're receiving; but different people's eyes could see this skin's colour differently. (And what of other animals' eyes? I've heard that parrots, for example, see more colours than we do. Maybe our skin colours would look quite different to parrots than to us.) Lighting conditions matter, too. In strong sunlight, much skin tends to have a lighter colour. Even some skin that's usually called "brown" looks quite pale in bright sunlight. So, what single colour does such skin really have? Which lighting is correct? Which eyes are correct? (We describe people as "white," "brown," "black," and so forth—noticing distinctive shades of skin colour. How accurate are we being? Maybe we're using simplistic labels, ones we don't really know to be applicable.)

Indeed, if no eyes were looking at this skin, would it have a colour at all? Looking at it, I see a colour. Then I look away, forgetting what I was seeing. Do I know that the skin's colour persists when I'm not seeing it? In everyday conversations, this question would sound crazy. (Yet are everyday conversations the ultimate arbiter of truth and rationality? Surely not. They contain much sloppiness of expression and reasoning.) I've often heard the famous philosophical question of whether, when a tree falls in a forest without anyone being there to listen, a sound is produced. Perhaps there's no sound as such when no one's ears are helping to produce an experience of a sound. All that would exist is the *potential* ("Just Add Attentive Ears") for a sound as such to exist. Is my skin also like that? Maybe it lacks all colour when no one's eyes are helping to produce an experience of its having a colour. (In the dark, if everyone is asleep, does skin lack colour?) Maybe my skin has no actual colour, possessing only potential colour. It might have only a potential to be interacted with by eyes, with this producing a colour-being-seen, the only kind of colour it can have. (And again, whose eyes are vital here? Mine? Other people's?) Is that what I'm like, in this respect? This is a disconcerting question. How may I answer it without being dogmatic and unreflective? I'm unsure.

So far, then, I'm struggling to know my physical nature. Maybe a scientist could do so, but I am no scientist. (Anyway, just like me, scientists rely on observation.) Nor is that the way in which, day by day, casually, I try knowing my body. Surely I should be able to know, by myself and without help, what is my own body. I should know, directly and without being assisted by others, where my own body begins and ends—exactly how much of the world's available space I occupy with my body. (It might matter to a pregnant woman, for instance, to know what is, and what is not, her body. What precisely does it include? This could be particularly relevant if she is open to the idea of having an abortion, only if she would be "exercising my right to control my own body." What *is* a person's "own" body?)

> *Surface question.* Does never being able to see through people's skin make life bearable? Is the inability to "look inside" other people's minds similarly helpful?

1.8   Family photographs

It's even more difficult for me to have that kind of knowledge about my body as it has existed over time, from one moment to the next. I take that for granted. I shouldn't, though. This is an important kind of bodily self-knowledge—as well, I suspect, as being surprisingly hard to have. Why might that be so?

I think I've had this body for many years. That's how people routinely talk about their bodies. But are we speaking carefully enough? Even if I now have a particular body, did this same body exist 35 years ago? Officially, I'm significantly older than 35. Was this body therefore also part of the world 35 years ago (answering to the same name I use now)? This one differs greatly from the earlier one. I began life with purely blonde hair, which later became dark; and obviously a man's face is not a boy's: aging alters many details. If I were to see the earlier body in photographs, I probably wouldn't recognize it—without prompting—as this one. I cannot see this one "in" it.

Similarly, if I were shown a picture (with no accompanying explanation) of me-as-I-will-be-in-twenty-years-time, I mightn't recognise it as me. I probably cannot see myself "in" it. Moreover, that body doesn't exist now, whereas this one does. Hence, how can they be the same body? Even if there's a similarity, perhaps it's between two different bodies, much as two siblings, or a parent and child, can resemble each other. In that sense, possibly the later person (portrayed in the picture) is *simply not me*—because I'm here now, not already existing later than now.

Equally, how can the earlier body—the 35-years-past body—really be me? It doesn't exist any more, whereas this one does. Nor do I remember having that earlier body. I certainly don't remember it *as* the photographs show it. If it was indeed an earlier stage of a continuing overall-body (with this present body being one stage of that continuing body), then at the time when it existed I was looking *out* of it. I wasn't beside or in front of it, looking *at* it. Nonetheless, the photographs show the earlier body only *from* beside or in front, only as it's being looked at—which isn't how I ever experienced it when the photographs were being taken. (I wasn't looking at my body from beside or in front at those moments; I was using it, in front of the camera.) Consequently, if no one had ever told me that the photographs are of me, I couldn't have known that they are. This makes my grasp of having such a past remarkably fragile, with that grasp depending on my being told stories about it, stories that need never have been told to me.

How trustworthy is my memory of my body's persistence anyway? I seem to have memories from when I was young—running, throwing, falling, and so on. How do I know that those *apparent* memories (as I should say if I'm speaking carefully and cautiously) are of this particular body's adventures? In a way, I don't have that knowledge—because, again, the earlier body is quite different to this one. I might think that it's continuous with this one, that it developed into this one. Yet have I meticulously observed—have I kept careful observational track of—the continuous development of that body into this one? Not really: over the years, I've slept a lot, I've paid attention to much else instead, and I've forgotten a great deal. As I said, I believe that no major transition between different bodies occurred along the way, when I wasn't paying attention; do I *know* that none did?

I realize how far-fetched that question sounds. However, could a person either be, or "own," a composite of different bodies—first one, then another, next a third, followed by a fourth, and so forth? These would "add up" to one overall-body. We might wonder when the "breaks" would occur between these various bodies. Would it happen overnight, yesterday's body being followed by today's, to be succeeded by tomorrow's, and so forth—all of these somehow being a single body? We might wonder how many of these "briefer bodies" a life would include—with a particular overall-body being constituted from the "briefer bodies" over time. Maybe there are several, even many, moments in "a single" life when a transition occurs between one body and a significantly different one. We're rarely, if ever, aware of this happening at the time. Still, one observes dramatic differences between how one's body is now and those earlier bodies; and one would infer that those differences must have come into existence at *some* time or other, even at many times. I'm not saying there are single seconds or minutes during which major body-swaps must have happened. But could there have been some notable days or months, when one body has replaced another within a single overall-body?

Day by day, I notice few changes. They're gradual; none seem worthy of comment (if I'm lucky). They add up, nonetheless, to dramatic differences. Suppose I could close my eyes (without hurting myself) for 10 years at a time. (Some Indian sadhus—unworldly ascetics who often impose extreme hardships upon themselves—undertake feats like this.) Suppose that I would open them, every 10 years, to see myself for 10 minutes—and either to rejoice or, more likely, to recoil from the changes.

"Is that me? Surely not. So different from last time!" It would be like a 10-yearly school reunion, with myself the only person attending. "Is that what I've become?" I wouldn't recognise myself!

This thinking is unsettling, although not unfounded. After all, we aren't always aware of everything occurring within us. To take one example: I've had occasional moments of "blacking out." When I emerge from one of these moments, looking around, at first there's no sense within me of having a past; I don't even see this body as mine. Then the moment passes (and I have little idea as to how long it has lasted). My life returns; or so I feel. Now a body is seen as mine. Some understanding seems to return—with a sense of myself, my body, and the world being handed back to me. However, perhaps "I" have changed, even physically, in the meantime. I look at my hand; at least, I look at a hand; only now do I begin thinking, "That's my hand." Having not thought of it as mine, now I do. Is this a return to self-knowledge? I want to believe so; but how do I suddenly gain—regain—the knowledge that it's *my* hand? Possibly, those moments of "rejoining" the world, when my gaze includes no sense of some body as being mine, are the moments of accuracy and insight. Perhaps they're the times when I have knowledge, even if it isn't knowledge of having a physical self as my own. (Does this sort of possibility also arise when people emerge from general anaesthesia, say?)

> *Timely question.* How likely is it that some form of reincarnation is true? What evidence is there of its truth?

1.9 My brain

Have I been overlooking something quite significant that science might tell me? Scientifically, it could seem, my *brain* is vital to being who I am. Would science claim that a specific brain—this one—is what makes me *me*? Does *its* continued presence sustain this body's being mine over time?

It's tempting to say so; would I know so? It's possible that at least some brain cells die, being replaced by new ones. (I've been told that, according to current scientific research, this happens to the rest of the body's cells—and might well do so, for some or all sorts of brain cells.) If it does happen, then this brain—this stuff—*hasn't* had a continued presence from my childhood until now, in that the brain cells inside this head wouldn't have been here 20 or 30 years ago. (Indeed, is this even the same *head* as was present those years ago? The "head cells" in general are being replaced!) Hence, it's possible that no continuing brain exists, constituting a continuing me. (Casually, I speak of its being "my" brain all along. But maybe I'm simply presuming there being an independent way of identifying myself as already existing, already in position to possess a brain. That sounds odd.)

I've also heard it suggested that some specific *area* of this brain might constitute me. Could it be "the seat of my consciousness"? I'm unsure that this suggestion avoids these philosophical worries, though.

For a start, perhaps cells within this smaller area of the brain also die, being replaced time and again. Possibly, there are no persisting special-area brain cells. I cannot persist due to a special-area-of-the-brain's doing so—if in fact it doesn't.

In any case, is it clear whether a person's fundamental identity is constituted by a brain's location, let alone by a special part of the brain being wherever it is? I might imagine a brain transplant, switching brains between two bodies. If my brain were inserted into a teenager's body, would that be me? (Would I be young again—an old head on young shoulders?) Then I might imagine, instead, just these brains' "special areas" being swapped. If my "special-brain area" was grafted into a teenager's brain, would that person be me?

Gosh. This is becoming rather befuddling.

Brain question. Is it conceivable that brain research reveals nothing about selves? Can we test this idea?

1.10   A motivational moment

These are odd thoughts, puzzling ideas, even perplexing ones that could test conventionally defined sanity. May I reassure myself by recognizing that I can ignore such thoughts, proceeding with a normal, less reflective, life?

That reassurance could be shallow and brief, though. By relying upon it, I could well be living a life based only upon *self-belief, not self-knowledge*, as to what I am. That wouldn't be good enough, I think. It could involve self-deception, for instance—a dangerous habit. Still, I must take care not to close my mind to unusual thoughts. Why so? Simple: I want to understand myself as well as I can, not merely to feel as if I'm doing so. Consequently, I'll continue seeking philosophical self-knowledge; and even if more odd ideas await me, I mustn't shy away from them simply because they're unusual. (Philosophical self-knowledge is unusual itself, I suspect.)

> *Motivation question.* What could prompt a person to want no self-knowledge? Can they know this about themselves?

1.11   Overview of the day

Before going to sleep, I'll take a moment to organise today's thoughts. There have been ideas, questions, objections, and doubts. Throughout, generating and accompanying these, there has been a shifting and complex pattern of reasoning. My understanding of it will be aided if I organise it a little ("after the event"), summarizing some of the day's main thoughts. (I'll do the same at the end of each other day in this adventure.)

Main question being asked:

> Do I know myself, in the sense of knowing what I am?

Main hypothesis (to be tested):

> I can know something of what I am, by knowing my own body. (I know myself as a physical presence within the world—as a being with a particular body, my own.)

Chief guiding questions and accompanying suggestions (arising while testing that main hypothesis):

> Can I ever know that a particular body is mine, by knowing its mine-ness at a specific time?
>
> *Suggestion:* Maybe I can do so by knowing the mine-ness of parts of this body at a specific time.
>
> Yet how can I know the mine-ness of a whole body by knowing the mine-ness of parts of a particular body, unless I already know the mine-ness of the body *containing* those parts at that time?
>
> *Suggestion:* Maybe I can know the mine-ness of a single *continuing* body, existing over a longer time.
>
> But how can I do that, given the dramatic changes that seem to affect bodies over time?

As I think back over today's musings, such questions assist me in clarifying the structure of my reasoning. Then a few further questions occur to me:

> Do you know your own body, in part by knowing other bodies? If your body were significantly different to other people's, would you struggle to know your body as being a person's body at all? ("It's *a*

body. Is it a person's body? It's mine. Yet it's so different to others I see, at the shopping centre, the beach, university, everywhere else. *They're* human bodies. Might this body not be a person's, then? Might I not *be* a person, compared to these clear-cut people gliding contentedly along?") Yet might everyone be thinking along such lines? Might everyone be wondering whether he or she is a person? Could a capacity for such self-questioning be part of *being* a person?

FURTHER READING

Today, I've attempted to *begin* thinking philosophically about my self, seeking knowledge of it. Have my questions and suggestions been the final word on how one might usefully ponder these issues? Surely not. So, I also want to encourage readers to engage with further, more complex, philosophical writings—with *others'* attempts to reflect upon such matters. Here are some possible readings of which I've become aware.

In Plato's dialogue *Apology* (at 38a), Socrates claimed—setting a philosophical agenda for the ages—that the unexamined life is not worth living for a person. René Descartes's *Discourse on Method* (1637), Part I, describes a similar motivation. There is also an enduring temptation to link the idea of self-examination with self-improvement. §1.1 introduced this link; for some related thoughts, see Crispin Sartwell, *Obscenity, Anarchy, Reality* (Albany: State University of New York Press, 1996), chapter 1.

Upon what *details* might a profitable self-examination first focus, then? In §1 of *On Certainty* (Oxford: Blackwell, 1969), Ludwig Wittgenstein said that "If you do know that *here is one hand*, we'll grant you all the rest." He was responding to G.E. Moore's infamous attempt, in the final pages of his "Proof of an External World"—see his *Philosophical Papers* (London: Allen & Unwin, 1959)—to prove the existence of the world in general, by showing how he knew of his having hands.

What could be simpler? Except that it isn't at all simple. Today (Day 1) began similarly, with me trying to know a hand as mine—and I soon encountered problems. §1.2 asked about how bodily *mine-ness* is to be known; on this, see P.F. Strawson's *Individuals* (London: Methuen, 1959), pp. 87-94. There are puzzling details. §1.4's questions fit with Descartes's observation—in "Meditation II" of his *Meditations on First Philosophy* (1641)—that, when seeing another person, strictly speaking he sees only "hats and coats which may cover automatic machines." He *infers*—not knowing conclusively—that there is more besides. (Why need the investigation become so demanding? §1.5 hearkens back to Descartes's *Discourse on Method*, Part II.) §1.6's example, of looking at oneself in a mirror without knowing who it is, comes from John Perry's "The Problem of the Essential Indexical," reprinted in Quassim Cassam (ed.), *Self-Knowledge* (Oxford: Oxford University Press, 1994). §1.7 directed us to subtleties raised by a classic philosophical distinction, between primary and secondary qualities. For a famous defence of the distinction, see John Locke's *An Essay Concerning Human Understanding* (1690), Book II, chapter 8. For an equally famous critical response, see George Berkeley's *Principles of Human Knowledge* (1710), §§9-15.

Personal identity *over* time entered here (in §1.8) via talk of bodily changes. For general thoughts, see Derek Parfit, *Reasons and Persons* (Oxford: Oxford University Press, 1984), §85. For sceptical thoughts, see Peter Unger's "Why There Are No People," *Midwest Studies in Philosophy* 4 (1979), 177-222. For a non-sceptical view, see Peter van Inwagen, *Metaphysics*, 2nd edition (Boulder, CO: Westview Press, 2002), chapter 11.

§1.9's idea of there being one personally re-identifying piece of the brain is defended by Roderick Chisholm: "Is There a Mind-Body Problem?", in *On Metaphysics* (Minneapolis: University of Minnesota Press, 1989). On the possibility of brain "swaps" (also mentioned in §1.9), see Sydney Shoemaker, *Self-Knowledge and Self-Identity* (Ithaca, NY: Cornell University Press, 1963), pp. 23-25.

And for wide-ranging questions about the self, the body, and the brain, see Daniel Dennett's "Where Am I?", in Dennett and Douglas Hofstadter (eds.), *The Mind's I* (New York: Basic Books, 1981).

KNOWING ONE'S MENTAL NATURE

And how reliable can any truth be that is got
By observing oneself and then just inserting a Not?

W.H. Auden, "The Way"

2.1 "The real me, the inner me"

A new day; new energy; a new idea. When I awoke this morning, I didn't open my eyes for a while. I was taking no chances: no ghostly hand floating before me would be allowed to bedevil me, inviting me to wonder whether it was mine. This time, upon waking, I just *thought*—staying still, quiet, listening ... to what? To my own thoughts. To my mind. To ... yes, me—the inner me. Listening, I said—silently, to myself—"This is the real me." Maybe (as yesterday suggested) I should be unsure how to know myself by knowing a body as mine. But surely I *can* know myself by knowing a mind. This one. The one producing these thoughts. The one responsible for yesterday's thoughts, even the doubts. It's active, it's alert, it's alive; and it's knowing itself, right now.

With that thought, I feel renewed confidence that I do know myself. Perhaps I'm knowing an inner self. After all, even when reclining in bed, eyes shut, I knew *something* called "me." And no one else could know it, certainly not in this way. It's hidden from them. Not from me, though. Not from itself. So, as I sprawl thoughtfully in bed, can I come to know myself, the real me, even more fully?

People talk of what they're "really" like, their nature "deep within." In each case, I suppose, the real person is being taken to be an inner person, a mentally inner person. Does this imply that the real person is only ever knowable *to* himself or herself, *as* a mind? Perhaps I am knowable only as a mind, and only to myself. Maybe self-consciousness is the key here. These are tempting thoughts. (It's not that the body I examined yesterday was not real; but was it clearly *knowable as me?* Yesterday left me unsure.)

People are even more tempted if they begin labelling their inner self a *soul.* More than that; they often term it "spiritual." It tends to be regarded as unique to us as people, elevating us morally above other animals.

Anyway, I'll now start thinking about the main idea in this—the idea of there being an inner me that's mental, that could be the real me, somehow special. Can I know this idea to be true?

> *Depth question.* How precisely can the depth of a person's character be measured? Or is there simply "deep" and "shallow"?

2.2   A non-physical me?

If I know my own mind, presumably I'll do so by knowing particular aspects of it. Which ones? How about some of its *actions?* I would know my mind by knowing what it does.

I'll begin testing that idea. What is my mind doing right now? Quite a lot. I'm focussing on a philosophical issue; wondering whether I have some knowledge of myself; contemplating a few possibilities, while asking whether I can have self-knowledge I'm hoping to have; and even proposing a form that such knowledge might take. These are mental activities. So, do I have some self-knowledge by reflecting upon this flurry of mental activity—if only by being aware of its happening at this moment? Maybe I know what my mind is currently doing: it's focussing, wondering, contemplating, asking, hoping, and proposing. Fine; then I may reach confidently for this reasoning:

> Right now, I am thinking in various ways; and I know this. Hence, I know myself *as* this thinker at this moment. Because I know I'm thinking, I know I exist, at least as this thinker. I have *this* self-knowledge.

Perhaps I can even strengthen that conclusion—by inferring that I know myself *only* as a thinker, not something physical. Even if (as yesterday's efforts seemed to show) it mightn't be simple to know bodily movements as my own, surely mental activity is different. When it's mine, I won't be able *not* to know it; and I'll know it, partly *because* it isn't physical. Suppose I try to doubt its being mine, testing whether I really know it. I would still know of this doubting; and to doubt something is to be thinking. So, this thinking—the doubting—would be known by me as more mental activity (like the wondering, the contemplating, and so on). I've heard that René Descartes, the seventeenth-century French philosopher, famously adopted this way of trying to know himself. This sort of reasoning, he thought, showed that his real, ultimately knowable, self was a non-physical thinker.

Yet *is* such knowledge readily available? Maybe I can test this by trying, right now, to ignore all sensory input. Even if I have no sense of whether I'm sitting, standing, running, walking, sweating, and the like, might I know I'm *thinking*? Perhaps I'm doing less with my mind, when concentrating on being a pure, sensorily deprived, mind. Whatever little activity is occurring, however, can be known.

All right, then, I'm testing that—striving to *make* my mind aware only of itself, thinking. Let's see ... I am imagining a weird weightlessness, as I try "withdrawing" my mind from sensory awareness.... I think I'm succeeding a little.... But I'm also becoming unsure that, if I were deprived of all sensory input, I could continue having that earlier knowledge of my thinking—my focussing, wondering, contemplating, and the rest of those efforts. The reason is simple. Because it's a mental *effort* to imagine the lack of sensory input, I am forced to stop musing on those other ideas. Never mind: I still manage to have some knowledge—because at least I know I'm making this effort! (Having said that, though, I should acknowledge that there has been research into sensory deprivation, including what effects it has upon a person's cognition. It isn't obvious that, in such circumstances, the mind retains calm control over itself. Even knowledge *of* one's thinking mightn't be easy to have as a "pure" thinker.)

> *Non-physical question.* Must there be something desirable in being non-physical?

2.3   Another methodological moment: introspection

Yesterday was odd. Careful thinking made me puzzled, even about what seems to be my own body. Will my mind be easier for me to know than my body has been?

Maybe; maybe not. How can I know in advance of trying? After all, prior to yesterday I didn't regard my *body* as difficult to know. Only now am I approaching my body *or* my mind so philosophically—so carefully and thoroughly.

Today, especially, I'm using what I believe the history of philosophy calls *introspection*. To introspect is to pay close mental attention to one's thinking. Not only am I thinking about myself; I'm recording this thinking, trying to decide when it's accurate. Can I gain knowledge of important aspects of myself, by monitoring my own thinking in that way? Might I know myself by knowing my mind?

> *Introspective question.* Could I think about my thinking about my thinking about a duck?

2.4 Listening to one's mind

Claiming to be non-physical is easy. The depth, the mystery—it's rather a thrilling prospect to contemplate; but is it also accurate? I routinely describe myself as thinking various thoughts. Yet how can I ever know that my mental experience is non-physical? Are all conscious thoughts obviously non-physical? Do I feel the non-physicality of my thoughts?

Suppose that, within my mind, unheard by anyone else, I form the words "I'm thinking." I don't speak them; I think them. Whether I thus create something non-physical depends upon what it takes for something to be non-physical. Here's one obvious suggestion: something is non-physical if it cannot be sensed or observed—seen, touched, and the like. Well, I cannot literally—with my hands—touch my experience of thinking those words, "I'm thinking." Nor can I see, taste, or smell the experience. Am I therefore unable to sense my producing those words, in the ways that physical things in the world around me typically are sensed? Does my thinking pass this simple test for being *non*-physical?

Not clearly. I *can* sense my consciously using the words, it seems. I can hear them ... not being said, but being thought. Yes, I don't hear them coming from another person. Only "within" me do I hear them. Still, isn't this a way of hearing something? Even if it isn't how I would hear someone else's words, maybe I sense my own differently. (It's as if I hear myself talking to myself.) Perhaps the words have a physical presence, then, within me.

How could that be so? I cannot use my other senses to trace this inner sound back to something else I can observe. That is, I cannot cross-check the sound against input from another sense. (Doing so is a natural technique. For example, I find—see and touch—the tap responsible for the irritating "drip, drip, drip" in the dark kitchen at night.) Notably, I cannot *see* or *touch* my brain's producing the inner words, "I'm thinking." But is that cross-checking required? The process I'm aware of might still be purely physical. Something's being physical doesn't guarantee its being accessible to more than one sense, does it? (I hear music—which is at least partly physical—even though I don't smell, touch, taste, or smell it.)

It's true that there are limits to how precisely I can locate this inner sound. Where, exactly, is it occurring within me? No specific position is being occupied by it, as far as I can tell. Imagine how crazy I would seem to others if I was saying to them, "I'm hearing those words within me ... where? ... over here ... no, over there ... no, no, two inches to the left ... a little more ... that's correct ... there they are." People would describe me as "hearing voices." I would reply, "Not quite. I'm hearing my own voice." But again, exactly where within myself would my own voice, those inner sounds, be occurring? Closer to my left ear than to my right? How near would they be to the top of my head? Would they be barely behind my eyes? I suppose that if the inner sounds aren't physical, then they do not literally occur somewhere, in some place. Once more, though, what is the evidence for their not being physical? I don't see why, because I cannot find an exact location for those thoughts, they must be non-physical. Nor do I concede that, because other people cannot hear my thoughts, these have to be non-physical. It isn't apparent that the world needs to guarantee the precise locatability by humans of everything physical within it.

Anyway, up to a point it feels as though I *can* locate those sounds of my thinking. I do this somewhat roughly, but perhaps well enough. For (and I know how simple this sounds!) the thoughts certainly feel as if they're inside my head. Is this some evidence for those inner sounds, hence for my thinking, being physical? Surely so. If my thinking is in my head, and if my head is physical, so is my thinking. (Otherwise, is my head partly non-physical?) My thinking also seems to occupy time, not only space: it begins and ends at particular times. So, I shouldn't be assuming that my thinking is non-physical. I can't reach out to touch my thoughts; nor can I see them. Yet this needn't prove that they aren't physical. In any case (as I've noticed just now), there is some direct reason for thinking that my thoughts *are* physical. (If they are, maybe another person, such as a neuroscientist, will be able, one of these days, to know I'm thinking on some occasion. Presumably, he or she would do so by observing what my brain is doing. I'll think more about this, sometime later.)

> *Consciousness question.* How mysterious is consciousness? Could there be a science of consciousness?

2.5   Discovering myself? Creating myself?

Maybe my thoughts are physical; maybe not. In either case, I'm puzzled about the idea of their being or constituting the real me. *Which* thoughts would do this? All of them? Only some? How can I know which ones are doing so? Still, I'll put that worry to one side for now, while concentrating on a related conundrum, a pivotal one for this enterprise.

Suppose that, trying to describe the real me, I commune for a while with my thoughts—writing down what I'm feeling, what I'm debating and proposing, and so on. Then I hesitate. I pause, realizing that, from here onwards, I cannot avoid taking a stance on how to answer the following questions:

> Is this record of my "inner life" *revealing* or *discovering* what I'm really like? Or is it *creating* or *constituting* me? (Perhaps my thinking uncovers a pre-existing and continuing inner reality, complete and unchanging, that makes me who I really am. Alternatively, maybe my thinking brings into existence the inner reality that makes me who I really am, a reality that changes as the thoughts change.)

Gee. That's quite some choice.

The first picture—the *Self-Discovery conception*, I'll call it—fits well with the belief that my identity is provided by a real self contained within me. A vital part of what I really am, the real me, would be something underlying my thinking, perhaps helping to generate my conscious ideas and feelings—but unable to be changed itself by how I think and what I do. Would those ideas and feelings at best *reveal* the existence and some of the nature of that independent inner self? Hopefully so; but this mightn't always occur. There's a chance of that pre-existing core, that inner me, having a character *beyond* my conscious awareness of it.

What of the second picture, which I'll name the *Self-Creation conception*? According to it, the real me *is* my conscious thinking—my ideas and feelings. There won't be any real me beyond my thoughts, generating and transcending them. The true me would be whatever I consciously do as a thinker. Different thoughts would constitute a different me! I would be in flux—the real me being altered as new thoughts arrive and depart.

That's a difficult choice between two ways of thinking about myself—the Self-Discovery picture and the Self-Creation story. Is there an underlying inner ... what is it? An inner person which is the real me, maybe shaping how I think? Or do I exist more "at the surface" of my conscious thought, with the real me *being* (rather than shaping) how I think? The Self-Discovery story could well accord me deeper reserves of potential thought, such as unconscious mental dispositions that will never be activated. On the Self-Creation story, I probably have no hidden depths like that. Rather, the real me just is my conscious mental life; and I'm created as my thinking is created, because I *am* the thinking. I *am* my consciousness.

Each of these possible images of myself sounds attractive; but can I rationally embrace both? Two significantly different ideas are being presented. People repeatedly seek to adopt both kinds of self-image—talking of their deeper, underlying selves, *and* of being able to alter themselves by their thinking (such as by "raising their consciousness," or by their "power of positive thinking"). Yet I'm unsure that the combination is coherent.

The problem is like one that puzzled me yesterday. I was pondering people's predilection for self-improvement, their wishing to "be all that they can be." I wondered whether such thinking can coexist sensibly with people already being wonderful, as they are often led to believe they are. People often proclaim proudly, almost as a mantra, how they're able to create and recreate themselves anew. Unwanted faults are left behind: "I've put that way of thinking behind me. I've moved on." A fresh person emerges: "I can be who I want to be. I'm a new person now." Fine; but should such talk be interpreted literally? (And if so, does *death* by improvement thereby occur—the former person dying, a new one being created?) *Can* an unchanging inner real me underlie my thinking, even as a new, alterable, real me is created by my conscious thinking? How could *both* of these be the real me?

A basic transformation in oneself is feasible, it seems, only if selves are created, not discovered, by conscious thinking. By thinking along new lines, I'm a new person, at least to some extent. Yet if I also have a real self waiting to be discovered, not created, by my conscious thinking, maybe there are limitations upon how much self-change I can undertake. Even if my "surface self" starts thinking in a new way, this won't guarantee my "underlying self" (if there is one) being changed. A surface "makeover" of my conscious thinking could involve my adopting new thinking about lots of issues; but that wouldn't ensure any underlying, or deeper, self within me undergoing a comparable "makeover." Deeper instincts could survive all changes in behaviour and appearance.

So, how different may I sensibly seek to become by altering my consciousness? How much of the real me could be improved in that way? Often, I've been exhorted to think more optimistically: "Be positive!" The idea usually seems to be that, by doing this, I'll make myself a more optimistic person. ("By thinking like that, you'll be like that. The more you think like that, the more you'll be like that.") This makes sense if the real me gets created by how I think—if the real me just *is* my conscious mental activity. However, what if crucial aspects of the real me are located beyond the day-to-day reach of conscious manipulation? Then real self-improvement is very difficult, maybe impossible. In contrast, if my consciously accessible thoughts are the real me, it's easier to improve as a person. I would need only to think better thoughts! ("Wait a moment: it's not always easy to alter how one thinks about some issue." That's true. In principle, though, it can be done; which is all I'm talking about at the moment.) Well and good; is that how I should proceed? It's what people advise. Yet they might be wrong about what people are really like, and therefore about what people can be like. *Am* I such a creation of my consciousness? If so, it's easier for me to change, "to grow and develop." By the same token, though, maybe I would lack the hidden mental depths that people tend to believe they possess. Perhaps I am somehow a *lesser* person if the real me can be altered so easily.

> *Creation question.* Could a person's identity be created more by others' thinking than by his or her own? Is it possible to derive most of one's thoughts from others? How unoriginal is it possible to be?

2.6   Partial people

I had better confront that idea, then, of being a lesser person (if I could be created afresh by thinking anew—"Change your thinking! Change yourself!").

Do I want to depend, for who I really am, upon what I actually think and feel? This sounds inviting, by implying that I can "take charge" of my thoughts and feelings. But there's a danger: I only think and feel *some* of the time on *some* issues (and not always insightfully, of course). So, if who I really am as a person is constituted by what my mind consciously does, won't I always be only *partially* a person? Maybe I would be extremely "gappy." Probably, I wouldn't notice my "gaps." I might even feel complete, a wholly capable and developed person. (Lots of people seem unaware of gaps in their thinking about life's subtleties.) Nevertheless, I would be only partly formed, due to my history of only-intermittently-attentive thoughts about just some aspects of life and the world. I would be much less formed than was possible.

This doesn't sound like a flattering way of describing someone. It isn't unrealistic, though. For a start, I'm not sure that anyone is fully formed, in that sense—being *all* that a person could be. Still, presumably some of us would be *more* fully formed than others; and many might be worryingly under-formed. ("This person votes?"—asked incredulously of someone who knows nothing of the issues, responding only to a candidate's looks, say.)

For an example of the less-than-adequately formed among us, think of those "celebrities" who reflect on little in the wider world beyond their physical appearance and money, their "life's journey," and so on. Tedious, shallow, narrow. (To be fair, they're probably no more incomplete than many others; but we hear them *ad nauseam* on radio, on TV, and so forth. Also, the mass communication media often portray these people as "role models.") For example, a 30-year-old movie or music "star" might still sound like a 16-year-old, having a few opinions indicating little thought, these being tiresomely repeated in one interview after another. The performer lives with few, if any, face-to-face criticisms of his or her half-formed views. (When, as occasionally happens, an "artist" does have considered beliefs about substantial matters, he or she might be widely lauded as a serious intellectual.) Maybe this kind of person *is* created, slowly, only as he or she develops, day by day, forming opinions purely when asked for them. The result: scant development of a real person. A caricature, little beyond the "media image," is formed. Accordingly, perhaps a genuinely and substantially incomplete person is what we hear whenever the "star" is interviewed. When young, I deemed such people "empty." Was I more literally accurate than I realized? Nor has my instinctive reaction to those people changed over the years. (If anything, I've become more conscious of how incomplete they are, as I have better evidence of what people *can* be like.) But now that reaction finds a philosophical home, fitting well with the Self-Creation conception of people. (Humility is needed, too. I should never forget that not only those people run this risk of being badly incomplete. Everyone does, myself included! Am I partly creating myself only now, via this philosophical questioning? I am what I think. I become what I think. If so, do I become nothing *beyond* what I think?)

> Choice question. Why do many people more readily see a need to improve themselves physically than mentally? Are most people more impressive mentally than physically?

2.7 An underlying self?

The alternative to the Self-Creation conception, it seems, is the Self-Discovery conception. According to it, some inner core, an inner self, underlies my conscious thinking. Throughout my life, I have sometimes assumed myself to possess an inner self like that. Certainly I've talked casually in that way. Was that self-image ever tested, though? Now that I'm really reflecting (rather than being content with everyday assumptions), I need to ask how I could *know* of an underlying self within me—situated beyond, and separate from, whatever thoughts I'm consciously having.

Whenever I search, via introspection, for a deeper and on-going self, I find only further active thinking. Nor should that be surprising: in introspecting, I'm using my mind actively; and this will hardly reveal part of my mind as existing-at-that-moment-*without*-being-an-object-of-my-active-consciousness. This combination is impossible. I cannot be actively thinking in a way that discovers a part of my mind not actively thinking. My discovering that part of my mind would involve its *thereby* being part of my conscious thinking. Hence, it seems, I cannot use self-reflection to discover hidden depths to my mind—bits of my mind not always, or ever, accessible to consciousness. I could never find such bits, because to find them is to find them *as* part of my being conscious! I cannot ever know *by* inspecting my mind, therefore, that some parts of it lie beyond consciousness. (The eighteenth-century Scottish philosopher David Hume noticed this profound sort of limitation.)

Here's another way of stating that point. When seeking some aspect of my mind—a real, underlying me—beyond my conscious thoughts, I couldn't know myself to be discovering something that was present *before* I consciously noticed it. My conscious investigation might even be creating it. Maybe it exists only as something being thought about; when I stop noticing it, perhaps it disappears! I might be making up ideas about myself while proceeding, rather than finding something already present within me, waiting to be discovered. So, no attempt of mine to find my inner self would prove the Self-Discovery view, defeating the Self-Creation interpretation of inner selves.

This general point can be better understood via interesting instances. For example, am I unable to know that, deep within, I'm a good person? The worry is that at most I would be conscious of having good thoughts—but even then, only *when* I'm thinking them. I couldn't be aware of any *further* Good Me underlying them. (I need to be actively good, therefore, if I'm to know that I am a good person. I could know of my goodness only by knowing of my being consciously good. Describing myself as good in some *hidden* way might be empty rhetoric. I'll try returning to this thought later.)

Possibly, then, I don't already have a separate self, lurking within me, complete with its own features. Maybe there is nothing to the real me beyond my conscious mind—my active thinking, my actual history of actual thoughts. (If so, however, I must keep in mind the danger, described above, of being too pliable, superficial, even incomplete as a person.)

Effort question. Should one's "real" self be knowable only with effort? Or effortlessly?

2.8 Whose thoughts are these?

I've attempted to know myself, the real me, by knowing my conscious thoughts. The problem with which I've been wrestling is that of knowing whether those thoughts are *revealing* the real me (an underlying inner self that already and independently exists), or whether they're *constituting* the real me (creating me while unfolding at the conscious "surface" of my mental life). Now here's a related, seemingly bizarre, question: how can I know that any of these thoughts are mine, deeply mine, in the first place?

Hmm. So, I try looking within my mind. Finding a thought, I assume it's mine. How do I know it is? Today I'm testing various thoughts, hoping these will either reveal or create the real me—thereby letting me know who I really am. All right; how can I, when confronted by a particular thought, know that it's mine, in the sense of belonging to a deeper me? If I don't already know who I really am (before noticing that particular thought), surely I don't know that the thought belongs to me—the real me. I could know that it's really mine, only if I already know who the real me is. I would be entitled to say only, "Here's an interesting thought. I wonder whose it is. Is it mine? Really mine? Deeply mine? I don't know, because I'm still working out who or what I am. Only once I succeed in doing that could I know whether any particular thought belongs to the real me." (And suppose I decide that this prior knowledge of who I am would require knowledge of a *body* as mine. Then yesterday's difficulties return.)

Admittedly, that sounds weird. I cannot read others' minds. Whatever thoughts I find must therefore be mine. Yes?

Yes ... and yet ... here is a lingering worry. Might some thought be mine only in a more shallow way? Could it be mine in a way that doesn't help to reveal, or to create, the real me? There are times when I want to insist that what I said or did (such as when unfairly causing a dispute) was not "the real me." Sometimes (I claim), it was an aberration, a passing and unrepresentative reaction. Overtiredness on my part, for instance, could warp my response to someone, leading to rudeness. Afterwards I might argue, in all honesty, along these lines: "You know that wasn't typical of me. It wasn't really *me* reacting. I'm sorry, really sorry."

So, the worry lingers. At any moment, is some particular thought helping to reveal, or to create, the real me only if it's a *typical* thought for me to have? Yet whether a given thought is typical for me might be difficult to know at the time. The challenge is to know which among the thoughts I experience *do* reveal, or create, the real me.

> *Individuality question.* Will we ever know how many typical ways there are for people to behave? Does all human behaviour fall into some understandable range of categories?

2.9 A persisting self?

That's an issue about knowing myself at a particular time. What about my existing *over* time? Is the real me some unique entity providing my fundamental identity from one moment to the next?

It's natural to say that, over time, I remain a *single* continuing thinker. I generate thoughts; later, I, the same I, might revisit them; even later, I, still the same I, can retain them. Throughout, a single, stably existing, mind persists; or so we usually believe. If I believe that my mental life at a particular time either reveals or creates my real identity at that time, presumably I'll believe that my mental life *over* time either reveals or creates my real identity over time, so that there is a single real me over time.

Yet recently I found some school exercise books from my primary school days (when I was 10 or 11 years old). Reading them, I had no sense of mental continuity with the consciousness that grappled with, and expressed, the thoughts written in those exercise books. ("Aren't you linked to them via a faculty of memory? Don't you remember writing them?" Good question. I'll think about memory in a moment.) These days, I cannot think as a child; in those days, I could not think as an adult. No one could ever, by examining those school books and my current consciousness, know that they belong to one person.

I'll try another approach, then. Can I *find*, in my thinking, the inner persisting me? Here goes: I am concentrating ... now ... trying to catch a thought happening ... now ... within me ... now ... and all the while trying to be conscious of myself persisting separately as the thinker.

Bother! Immediately there is a hurdle. What emerged just now was a succession of thoughts. Each instance of "now" was new, occurring at a slightly different time. Did I notice a single thinker having each of those thoughts in turn? Strictly, I noticed a few brief thoughts, each present at a new moment. Did I also notice a single thinker, the real me, being present at those various times? Ordinary conversations fall into the habit, in such situations, of assuming that a single inner person persists—existing throughout, linking the different thoughts. But at each of those new moments, I concede, my mind was "living in," being wholly present in, that new moment. No part of my mind was simultaneously "staying behind" with the earlier thought, so as consciously to link two moments at once.

Anyway, how could that ever occur? Time moves on, as does the active mind. I thought an instance of "now"; then I thought a new "now," followed by another. At each of those moments, perhaps, *a* "thinker," *an* "I," was present and having a thought. However, this doesn't prove that there was a *single* thinker of all of these occurrences of "I"—a single thinker who was present, having different thoughts in turn, at each of those moments. Maybe at only some of those times was the real me present. Could there have been a new thinker (each using the word "I") at each new moment?

That question sounds outlandish, until I reflect upon the following analogy.

Sometimes, when walking between home and my office, the daily sameness of the experience feels oppressive. I stand in the same spot, ready to cross the same road in the same way. Looking around, I'm conscious of how each day could, in that respect, be any one of many similar previous days. I cannot distinguish being in this place now from being in the same place exactly five years ago (as I might well have been). And although that way of describing the reaction sounds as if it should suggest the existence of a persisting me, it doesn't. I don't retain, within me at this moment, a sense of myself-five-years-ago. What was *then* my sense of a Me has departed. All I have is the present sense of myself. It is as if I'm a new Me in that place every day: I may as well be, as far as I can tell by consulting my consciousness.

This doesn't prove that there is no single continuing inner me. Still, it makes me question whether there is. Maybe my self as such is, at any time, only me *at* that time. Every day, literally a new self would awake. Might the idea of a single continuing self therefore be merely a convenient and simplifying fiction, a useful story we tell? It simplifies life, talking and thinking of oneself as a single persisting self—with this-self-now being part of the same overall self as some-self-at-an-earlier-time. That approach makes for smoother conversations with other people. Is there nothing deeper than that, though, in references to one's on-going inner self?

> Persistence question. Would it be bad not to have a single persisting inner self?

2.10   An unchanging inner self?

Sometimes people claim that each of us is, from start to finish, a single *and unchanging* mind. (Often, this idea accompanies a belief in each of us having an eternal soul, pure in its unchangingness, perhaps surviving beyond our bodily end.) A moment ago, I found that the singleness of my mind, considered as a self, shouldn't be taken for granted. What now of its being unchanging at its core? Do I know of my mind's having within it something unaltered, even unalterable? Has this "something" persisted throughout my life, binding me from moment to moment, keeping me *me*—an on-going person?

I began today's musings by supposing that my inner me is most likely to reveal itself through what it does, its activities. I would know of my mind by knowing what it's thinking, feeling, and so on. They are the mental activities I notice, and which I take to be my own. But here's an obvious truth: *they* change. Over time, they change in content, tone, maturity, insight, attitude, and so forth. So, how could they provide evidence for an aspect of my mind as a whole *not* changing? Imagine finding a recording of my thoughts and feelings from 30 years ago. Those I'm having now would have little in common, in their content, with the older ones. There might be no overlap at all in content. I wouldn't be tempted to regard two wildly different bundles of thoughts and feelings as belonging to a certain person today and that same person two days earlier. So, maybe I should be equally cautious about regarding two very different bundles of thoughts and feelings as constituting a single person over a *longer* period of time.

> Unchanging question. Do horses, for example, have unchanging inner selves? Do humanly-named horses (such as pets or racing horses) have such selves?

2.11 Memories

Some people say that memories reveal, or constitute, the internal continuing self. The idea is that, so long as I have my memories, I have my identity: as the seventeenth-century English philosopher John Locke might say, my memories of a life make it *my* life. I know who I am by knowing what memories I have.

Although that sounds promising, I'm not wholly reassured. I cannot remember much of my life. Most of it is now a blank or a blur to me. Furthermore, as I concentrate my energy into what I'm striving to do with my life, I focus more on the present and the future. When I try marshalling my memories, there are images, smells, sounds—and gaps. Not systematic ones, either; randomly scattered ones! Memories aren't going to give me *much* self-knowledge. (So, even if I were creating myself with them, a merely partial person might result.)

Indeed, I'm not sure they will give me *any* self-knowledge. Whenever I think I'm remembering some past event, how do I know I'm really remembering? How do I know that my experience is actually a process of remembering, not of imagining? In order to have this knowledge, I need to know that the thought—the image, the aroma, the emotion—is really mine, for a start. (Otherwise, it only *seems* to me to be a real memory of mine. It would feel like a real memory, an accurate portrayal of what really occurred, as experienced by me. However, it wouldn't be a real memory; it would *only* feel like one.) It's far from clear that I can have that further knowledge.

Here's why. Earlier, I noticed the following difficulty about satisfying a similar requirement:

> Until I know who I really am, I don't know that a thought is really mine. (I would have to identify the thought as mine, partly by *already* knowing who I am. So, I cannot identify myself to *begin* with by knowing already that an encountered thought is mine.)

That seems to be a limitation on self-identification via *any* identified thoughts. Now I realize that the limitation also applies, more specifically, to any particular thoughts that feel like *memories*. Here's that application:

> I would have to identify a thought as one of my memories, by *already* knowing who I am. So, I couldn't identify myself to *begin* with, by knowing already that an encountered thought is a memory of mine.

This is a "chicken-and-egg" problem. Which of two possible pieces of knowledge would have to exist before the other could do so? Must I first know who I am? Or could I start by recognizing a thought as mine, before I know who I am?

It might sound odd to ask whether I know that an experience of mine that feels like a case of remembering something is really a memory of mine. Whose else could it be? Yes, except that I could sensibly question its being a genuine memory at all. Real memories are meant to be accurate records of a past part of a real life; and wouldn't I have to look beyond having the feeling, the inner experience, so as to verify its accuracy? We expect memories, it seems, to *discover* our real selves, not just to *create* some self or other.

Anyway, yesterday I acknowledged how often there are unavoidable breaks in memory: sleep gets in the way, as does inevitable inattention. Even if I have an inner self, therefore, would it cease existing whenever I'm not actively remembering? If remembering is necessary to a continuing inner self's being revealed or being created, presumably *no* continuing inner self is revealed or created much of the time—when I'm *not* remembering. In practice, I trust that whenever my apparent power of memory resumes duty, so does the same inner self as was previously at work. Yet how could I ever know, rather than merely trust, that this is happening?

> Memory question. Do some aspects of one's life need to be forgotten if one is to improve as a person?

2.12   A valuable inner self?

Would my inner self, if I have one, be *worth* having? As far as I can tell, when people assert that, buried deep within, there is a real self, they tend not to think of it only as supplying a "technical" identity. That could be achieved by a mere "thing," an "object," inert and featureless with the rest of the person built around it. No: people usually expect an inner self to have value in itself, possessing its own valuable properties. Often, they're thankful for having a real self like that, responsible for much of what is valuable in themselves.

Unsurprisingly, therefore, only rarely do people admit to being bad within their real selves. ("I curse my real self." Possible, although unusual.) Almost everyone, I suspect, would think that his or her inner self has many terrific properties. On that approach, if others don't see me as admirable, I need only tell myself how no one else appreciates the fine inner self that is "the real me." For example, how many people regard themselves as very unintelligent or as lacking all moral worth? Not many, I conjecture. Even when failing many exams, or when committing fraud or adultery, say, people might well console themselves with thoughts of the intelligence or moral worth located deeper within them. "My ultimate moral worth is my inner self," they might claim. So, if I'm to know my real self, maybe I should look for something inside me with those great qualities itself. Would this be how I have some of my most valuable qualities?

It's comforting to think so. Still, here's another thought. If my inner self is so significant in its details, is it correspondingly complex? There could be a price to pay for that. Presumably, a more complex inner self would also be *harder* to know. Because it would have more details, there will be more ways of making mistakes in trying to describe it (especially if I'm not simply creating it by *whatever* I think about it). Hence, by making more striking claims on behalf of the inner self I believe myself to have, I could be less likely to *know* that I have an inner self like that.

Undaunted, though, I'll spend a few moments assessing the likelihood of my having an inner self with some of those seemingly desirable qualities.

Value question. Is there a specific minimum degree of value that each person has, just by being a person?

2.13   Intelligence

Most people, it seems to me, are confident of having good intelligence. (I'm reminded of surveys that ask parents to rate the intelligence of their children. I seem to recall that around 80 per cent of the parents deemed their children to be smarter than average!) One popular thought is that everyone could be smarter "on the outside" if only we made the effort—because "on the inside" everyone is much more intelligent.

Such confidence is puzzling. Like anyone else, I've often acted stupidly, and on many occasions I haven't been smart enough to solve some intellectual problem. This makes me wary of regarding my intelligence too generously. Couldn't such generosity easily be mistaken? Do I know myself to be intelligent? This question is especially important for me, in my current quest for self-knowledge. To the extent that I'm not intelligent, I'm less likely to understand the issues—the questions, the puzzles, the possibilities—that arise in this search. (Just thinking hard mightn't help me, either. If I'm not very intelligent, I cannot escape this limitation when reflecting upon whether I am intelligent. Even if I decide that, yes, I am smart, I can still be an unintelligent person deciding this! Even if I feel that I'm understanding the questions, the puzzles, and the possibilities arising in my reflections, this feeling might be mistaken. Intelligence, let alone intellectual accomplishment, isn't simply a feeling.) There's a danger, then, of not being sufficiently intelligent when thinking about oneself.

Yet will everyone be open, intellectually and emotionally, to taking that danger seriously? Many people seem to regard it as part of being mentally healthy that one think of oneself as intelligent. (Isn't that part of what having high self-esteem is often meant to include?) "I'm not stupid," is a common refrain. (As if people's telling us that that they are not stupid proves they aren't.) "I'm no Einstein, but surely it's like this: ...," is the closest that many people will approach to an admission of having a limited, let alone faulty, intelligence. (Of course, this isn't much of a concession. Almost no one is as clever as Einstein—or, for that matter, as clever as Socrates, Plato, Aristotle, Descartes, Hume, Kant, and quite a few of the best-ever philosophers.) Indeed, it is revealing that people never describe their intelligence as "faulty." They admit only to being *less* bright than is possible or than some other people (such as Einstein!) are. But I don't want to evade this potential truth about myself. How can I know for sure that my mind isn't faulty? If a car were to make as many mistakes as my mind does, I would call the car faulty. Surely I should be no less demanding of my mind. (I might kick the car; I can't kick my mind. I could curse the car, though; and sometimes I curse my mind.)

Here's a deeper point. In order to assess my mind's quality, I must pay attention to its contents. What beliefs do I have? Which ideas are occurring to me? What distinctions am I making? What questions am I asking? These are questions I should ask, because the beliefs, ideas, distinctions, and questions in my mind are indications of whatever intelligence I possess. How far will answering those questions take me, though, towards knowing how intelligent I am? Not as far as I might have hoped. The problem is this. Even if it can be easy to notice one's having a particular idea, it is never easy to notice one's *not* having that idea. In fact, it is impossible. Of necessity, my noticing that I am *not aware* of X would involve my *being aware* of X: my noticing that I'm not aware of an eagle above me would have to include my being aware of the eagle! So, my noticing what is in my mind won't reveal to me what is absent from it. Moreover, I cannot accurately assess the intellectual quality of my mind unless I know, not only what is in it, but also what *should be* in it (yet is not). In other words, I cannot assess my mind's quality just by gazing inwards upon it. (I have a feeling, nonetheless, that many people do this when assessing their own intelligence. They think contentedly of what thoughts they have. Seemingly, they forget that there are other thoughts—better ones, quite possibly, even ones they should have—that they lack. Some of these other thoughts could be doubts about the truth of the thoughts they have!) Consequently, at any moment I would also need to look beyond my mind, increasing its contents. This will involve observing and thinking about the world, reading widely and well, being exposed to worthwhile new ideas, and so forth. Even then, there are no guarantees. If I'm not particularly smart, there is only so much I will learn or understand. Even if I were clever, there would still be limits to my mental capabilities.

Still, even if all such thinking about much outside my mind has limitations, it is *needed* if I'm to know myself as being intelligent.

(An analogy occurs to me. Think of people born to privilege, or who gain money and prestigious jobs partly through such unearned advantages as going to the "right" school, perhaps an expensive private one. Often they'll congratulate themselves upon their subsequent wealth and attainments, forgetting or never noticing the crucial contribution of their good luck. Such a person might be annoyed at any suggestion of not having earned their success: "Of course I've done so. I've worked hard." But many people work hard without being well rewarded. So the privileged person's hard work as such doesn't fully explain their success. Working hard in the right place at the right time—an opportunity available through the initial privilege—is more likely to be the story! Others could well have been better at the job, had they been given the chance. It mightn't be such a difficult job, either. Anyway, what's relevant to my reflections right now is that the privileged person who isn't mindful of his or her good fortune only notices what's within his or her mind, such as a sense of the work he or she has performed. Whatever isn't in his or her mind *but should be*—namely, an awareness that others, less privileged, might have done the job even better—is overlooked. Accordingly, the person doesn't clearly know how talented and intelligent he or she is, due to having that job.)

Intelligence question. Does intelligence ever reflect character? Is any of it ever earned, rather than genetically given?

2.14 Moral worth

Many people feel that their real self, their inner self, has a *moral* quality that mightn't be replicated in ways other people can observe. "I'm a good person, within myself," is the cry. Okay, then; perhaps I have an inherent moral worth just because I'm replete with well-intentioned ideas, reactions, feelings, and desires. (Often, we accord moral worth to other animals when we start seeing them as having similar mental complexity to us.) Possibly, there is goodness in everyone for that kind of reason! Can everyone know this about themselves? If so, then I can know it about myself, too.

I'm not sure about that, though. From where should I gain this confidence about my inner goodness? It's not obviously an innate belief, present in children from the outset. My impression is that this sort of belief in one's inner goodness wouldn't be in a child's mind until his or her parents, for instance, put it there: "You're such a good child. You really are." Yet how do *they* know this about the child? Perhaps it is more faith than knowledge. Conceivably, it is mainly encouragement! The child's short life, after all, has contained almost no opportunity to display unequivocal and sustained moral goodness. Reflecting upon myself, too, I concede that I don't see Goodness sitting inside me. I do not even know what it would look like. Nor do I *feel* its presence in some fool-proof way. I can try looking within myself (rather than merely believing others who might assure me of my inner moral worth). I'm not confident, though, about *where* such goodness would be located inside me.

Here's an alternative line of thought, then. Maybe my goodness (even if it's real) could never be wholly "inside" me. Perhaps, if I'm to know that I have moral worth, I need to watch what my body does, how I act "in the world"—looking beyond my inner self. If (to speak awkwardly) my body acts badly, I should admit that I'm being bad—and hence that I'm not so morally wonderful after all.

Or is this being too strict with myself, holding me-as-a-whole accountable simply to my bodily actions? In some circumstances, yes. I, the real me, might be morally innocent on a particular occasion if I had *resisted* performing the bad action, for instance. On the other hand, even this needn't be because the real me, with this inner desire not to perform the action, has a special moral worth. The reason would just be that if the desire were absent then the real me (the inner real me) wouldn't have been involved in the action's being performed. In this deeper sense, it wouldn't be *me* doing the bad action in the first place.

How good an explanation is that? This question takes me back to some of today's earlier passages of thought, about whether my thinking reveals or, alternatively, creates a separate real me. If I don't know that there *is* a real inner me like that, then I also don't know of myself as having a real inner me with notable, inherent, moral worth. (This "if ..., then ..." reasoning relies upon the following principle: If I don't know that an X exists, then I don't know that an X-with-the-extra-characteristic-Y exists—no matter what X and Y are.) I'm not saying I know for sure of my lacking those pieces of knowledge. It's a possibility to take seriously, though.

> *Moral question.* Do people gain or lose moral worth by their actions? Can this also occur through their thoughts?

2.15   *Personal values*

It could be emotionally difficult for me to cease believing in my having a real and significant inner self. Is this because such a self would house my deepest commitments, my personal values? Seemingly, I "store" them deep inside, locked into my mind (hopefully to be used, not just admired for being there: "Impressive: he has values!"). By believing strongly in these, potentially I make me—the deep, fundamental, me—who I am. If so, do I know myself in part by knowing which values I accept? Maybe I would therefore help to *create* myself, my real identity, by choosing among possible deep commitments? (Yet who or what *does* this choosing? Some commitments choose others, it seems. So, perhaps I am nothing *beyond* my most powerful commitments. Hmm.)

Even that suggested path to self-knowledge isn't so simple. Suppose I say I'm a pacifist, this being one of my deeply-held values. I could then have difficulty in knowing what this claim even means. Here's how I might initially attempt to analyse the claim: "It means my being opposed to war, calling it immoral." In all circumstances? "Perhaps it's morally acceptable only when waged in self-defence." Then what about when other innocents one knows are attacked? What about rushing to defend a valued and trusted neighbouring country that has been attacked without warning (while lacking sufficient defence capacity through no fault of its own)? "Maybe that's acceptable. It depends." On what? "On different possible details. On the particular circumstances." So you cannot say, exactly? "Not exactly."

That back-and-forth is only a start. What does it already reveal, though? It makes me realize I'm not offering an impressive defence, or even a significant statement, of my personal commitment to pacifism. So, the initial statement of my supposed commitment could be more like an opening attempt to outline a personal value than like a final considered position. Maybe I'll never be able to develop the opening statement into a coherent final position. (In practice, once people nominate something as one of their deep values, others tend not to ask them for details that might expose the commitment as vague and poorly understood. This reluctance can reflect tactfulness, a genuine desire not to make someone uncomfortable or to render a social interaction needlessly tense. Unfortunately, it can leave people thinking, contentedly but mistakenly, that they really understand their statements of commitment, even when these are quite vague or worse.)

Okay. If that example is indicative, there's a real possibility of my not knowing—at least not precisely—what my values are. This makes me feel awkward; but that unwelcome feeling must be accepted, not shirked. I have vague ideas, some general preferences, as to which values I want to endorse; and I can state these, vaguely and roughly. Still, I probably haven't thought through all these beliefs, covering every realistically possible circumstance or fully understanding the terms.

Of course, I could refuse to engage in such intellectual probing— insisting that I have a list of values (such as are given in one of the world's holy books); "and that is that," I might say. "Those are my personal values. *I* know what I mean and value, even if I cannot explain it to others." That response is quite dogmatic, however, with a fearful and strained quality. What's more, there is little point in reacting so dogmatically if, regardless of my inner confidence, I don't really understand my list. I should admit, I think, that this failing is possible. I want to know that I really understand my list of values, as against merely feeling or blindly insisting that I do.

In fact, I want something more: I hope the list is *right*. There can be a trade-off here, in terms of the self-knowledge at stake. The simpler the list, the greater my chances of understanding it—and thereby of understanding myself, as someone who identifies with it. Equally, however, the simpler the list, the greater the chances of it—and thereby of myself, identifying with it—being *too* simple to do justice to what seem to be the world's moral surprises, the world's moral complexities. Thus, I might have a better chance of knowing myself insofar as my values are simple; but I could be less *worth* knowing, if my values are too simple to be accurate in how they classify and react to the world.

> *Values question.* Why do people disagree so much over values? What does this show about people in general?

2.16 *Inner character*

There could be a related problem for my chances of knowing my character. Part of my knowing my character would be my knowing my personal values; which is not so easy, I've seen just now. Character is also action or behaviour, though; and knowing these can be complicated, I suspect.

Consider the example of bravery. Can I know I'm brave, simply by looking within myself? No. I need to know how I've acted in various situations. It isn't enough to pause for a moment, thoughtfully wondering whether I'm brave, then deciding I feel brave. This feeling might be transitory; it needn't be responding to anything genuinely threatening; in any case, it is only a feeling. (Many people, I expect, think of themselves as brave, based on nothing more substantial than that. Plus—in the case of some men—a flexing of muscles, maybe!)

Does this mean that I mightn't know whether I am brave? After all, I've rarely been called upon to be brave. My bravery, or lack of it, hasn't been sufficiently tested. So, I don't have much observational evidence. (Sure, situations have arisen where I have acted in ways that might indicate my being likely to act bravely if more demanding situations were to arise; but I said "might." Inferring that I'm brave, on the basis of those experiences, would be highly unreliable.) As the cliché says, "Actions speak louder than words." It's true. At least some self-knowledge, then, awaits actions which might never have an opportunity to occur.

What's true of bravery in that respect could also be true of much else. I might live a long life without ever knowing, for many potentially significant personal characteristics, whether I have them. In my early teenage years, I told myself that I would be a conscientious objector if the Vietnam War lasted long enough for me to be drafted into it. (I even began "practising" for prison—briefly putting myself onto a bread-and-water diet.) I felt that I had a personally pressing aversion to war in general—even apart from that particular war, which seemed unimportant to my own country's security. Did I know myself in that respect? It felt like I did, except that sometimes I wondered whether I was just reaching for a convenient excuse. Deep within, possibly I was just scared of battle. All my living male relations at the time had served in war. I had an informed sense of how awful it could be.

> *Character question.* Is a worthwhile character already needed, if one is to develop worthwhile character? Which aspects of character can arise afresh?

2.17   Free will

I've left unresolved the fundamental choice between a Self-Discovery conception of myself and a Self-Creation conception. Yet can I resolve that choice easily, by focussing upon another valuable quality that is often attributed to a person's inner self? Deep within us (goes the story) lives a special ability, traditionally called "free will." Living with a free will, I would rise above the merely mechanical world, a creature of spirit and inner enterprise. Living without a free will, I would be ... what? Maybe I'm little more than a leaf in the wind, a drop of dust on the sidewalk, if my real self lacks a free will. Alternatively, even if I'm somehow more than a leaf, I might remain less than a deeply free being. For instance, might I be no more free within myself than a baboon is?

Presumably, it depends upon what free will is. I've heard a few suggestions. One of them calls free will a capacity for using one's mind freely, debating alternative ideas or options. Then again, perhaps free will is one's being able to act even in ways which one will never actually pursue. Or it might be an aptness for being blamed or praised. (It makes sense to blame a person for a mistake. It is absurd to chastise a TV or a slug for an unfortunate outcome.) It could be our susceptibility to being morally responsible for what we do. Maybe it's some combination of these possibilities. In any event, it is significant, substantial. It is far from being a trivial or merely technical aspect of me.

Do I even use it to *make* myself whatever I am? Perhaps I freely "write" my life's story, even as I am living it. I've heard people claim that, with our free wills, we can create our inner selves. That is how deeply my free will would feature in my life. I would control how I live, by controlling what I *am* as I live. What limits would there be to this? Lots of people assert, with gusto, that there are no limits to our capacity to constitute, to shape and to reshape, ourselves. Those people are assuming that our real selves are our inner selves; and they're regarding inner selves as being eminently controllable. On that popular way of thinking, therefore, the Self-Discovery view amounts to nothing more than the Self-Creation view. So, the Self-Creation picture would be the paramount insight, explaining how we are what we are; then the implication would be that I discover what I am, only insofar as I create what I am. I would discover myself *by* creating myself. Whatever is created is all there would be to discover. The only underlying deep and persisting part of me would therefore be my free will, this capacity to control and to shape the rest of me.

Gee. If only it were that simple; but I doubt that it is. Surely questions from earlier today will remain, as to how I could know of a single, persisting, real, inner me—regardless of whether it's to be called a free will. Moreover, I'm not confident that my free will *would* be a wholly inner aspect of me. If it is, maybe I could come to know whether I have a free will by reflecting upon my thoughts and feelings, for example. Yet *is* having a free will simply a matter of having an appropriate feeling, say? Perhaps not, if free will is to be as substantial a quality as people usually claim. A feeling isn't very substantial. Yes, my feeling on some issue can matter greatly to me. Yes, it can make me do this, rather than that. But is a feeling a substantial *ability* or *capacity*? That doesn't sound quite right. For a start, surely I'll need the surrounding world to cooperate with any such feeling, if much is to be achieved (so that I have a useful ability or capacity). Real freedom—of a kind worth having, with which to remake the world and to travel unfettered through it—is a freedom within the wider world, not just within one's mind. (It is a freedom to act more widely, not only to think.) In that case, though, I would know that I have a free will only by looking beyond my mind, beyond my inner self. I'll need to take into account more than merely *feeling* free, for example. I wouldn't know of a free will's presence within me simply by searching my inner mental self.

So, there's a real choice to confront. If free will need only be comparatively trivial and insubstantial (such as a feeling), presumably I could know of it simply by experiencing it within myself. But in that event, so what? This knowledge would be *of* something comparatively trivial. (If that's all I am, of course, then well and good.) On the other hand, if free will is to be comparatively significant and substantial, it's likely to be something beyond just an object of consciousness (such as some thinking or feeling). It mightn't even be a wholly internal feature of a person. Maybe it's a combination, reflecting also how we function within the wider world; in which case, possibly there is difficulty in knowing when we're free in how we think and act. (This contemplated complexity in a will's being free would also make it harder for me to know that I *do* have a free will.)

Even talking of my having a free will, therefore, won't obviously show that the Self-Creation picture of myself is correct. Even a free will would need to be discovered, rather than created—which, to say the least, could be a difficult discovery to make! A free will might be present only insofar as the surrounding world co-operates; whether this occurs is not known just by gazing inwards upon one's mind. Nor is it wholly within one's control, created by sheer will-power.

> *Wilful question.* Could some wills be more free than others? Is a will free only if the associated body is?

2.18 A pause

How much, if any, of my mind is knowable by me? Today's thinking leaves me unsure. Yesterday's thinking had a similar effect. It left me uncertain about how much, if any, of my body I could know. So, where does my thinking, from these two days, leave me? Knowing neither my body nor my mind? Not knowing myself at all?

That's a disturbing prospect. Can I avoid it?

Maybe I'll need to spend time reflecting upon what knowledge is in the first place. I've been using the words "knowledge" and "know" without trying hard to figure out what, precisely, they mean. That's fine, if nothing much is at stake; but a lot is at stake here, and working out what those words really mean could be crucial. Still, perhaps the questions and doubts I've raised about my gaining various kinds of self-knowledge will be found *not* to drive away all self-knowledge—once I'm clearer as to what self-knowledge even *is*.

Right now, though, I'm not so confident about that. I'll therefore have to take seriously the caution contained in the following question: What is self-knowledge, *if* people ever have some? (Equally, what is it, even if they don't have any?)

Tomorrow, then, I'll try answering that question in a provisional or hypothetical way, putting to one side for a while the issue of whether I *do* have self-knowledge. Here's my plan. I'll reflect on the nature of knowledge in general and the nature of self-knowledge in particular. Once I find out what self-knowledge *would* be like (if I, for instance, were to have some), I can again attempt to decide whether I do have any; and, by then, my attempt will reflect more understanding of what I'm doing, of what I'm seeking.

Anyway, that's enough philosophy for today. I'm going to sleep, heartened by that plan. Tomorrow's focus will be on the nature of self-knowledge itself. Can I learn how to distinguish self-knowledge from whatever might only seem to be self-knowledge? If I cannot, then, ... no, I won't contemplate this possibility at the moment. It's hardly relaxing.

Question question. What *is* a question? Do all questions seek knowledge as their answers?

2.19   Overview of the day

Before I fall asleep, I'll take stock of today's reasoning. Roughly speaking, it had the following form.

Main hypothesis being tested:

> I can know myself by knowing my real self—an inner self, a mental self. (My self-knowledge is therefore quite different to what it would be if it were knowledge of my body.)

Chief questions raised (as part of testing that main hypothesis):

> Do I know that my mental self is not physical?

> Do I know my mental self as something already existing? Or do I know it as something I create by thinking about it?

If I'm to *create* my inner self as I proceed, maybe it isn't hard for me to know it. However, would *what* I know—that inner self—also be a lesser thing than it feels to me to be? In other words, would there be little *substance* to my real self?

If I'm to *discover* my inner self as something already existing, maybe it's more substantial. Yet would it therefore be *harder* to know?

For example, do I know of it as a single, unchanging, continuing, part of me? Do I know of it as an intelligent or morally valuable part of me, a home for my free will?

Indeed, would I know my inner self only, in part, by knowing aspects of the world *outside* my mind?

The following questions seem to flow naturally from some of my others.

> Can I ever disagree with myself at a single time? If I carefully contemplate two conflicting views, unsure as to which to accept, can I know before accepting either that only one of them would reflect who I really am? Would this be a good reason to accept the view in question? ("This one, not the other, fits with how I've always thought about the topic in the past.") However, might I always have been thinking about the topic in a way that wasn't true to the real me? (At what stage of one's life does a real person, a fully formed inner self, first emerge? Can there only be one real or true self within a life?)

FURTHER READING

Today started, in §2.1, with the idea that a person, most carefully considered, is something mental, not physical. The seminal philosophical source for this is Descartes's "Meditation II" (see yesterday's "Further Reading"). There, Descartes generates and elaborates upon a version of his celebrated thought, "I think, therefore I am." His reasoning has been honoured here, in §2.2, by similar self-examination. A contemporary, but difficult, defence of a mind's being non-physical is David Chalmers's *The Conscious Mind* (New York: Oxford University Press, 1996).

Descartes used introspection, an approach that was noted in §2.3; for discussion of introspection, see William Lyons, *The Disappearance of Introspection* (Cambridge, MA: MIT Press, 1986). Descartes's thinking led to the hypothesis of a person's ultimately being an *inner* mental self. §2.4 asked whether such an individual can be known simply by hearing it. On knowing an individual purely via sound, see Strawson's *Individuals* (London: Methuen, 1959), chapter 2. §2.5 distinguished between creating a self and discovering one—particularly a mental self. On this (paying special attention to emotions), see Charles Taylor's

"Self-Interpreting Animals," in his *Human Agency and Language* (New York: Cambridge University Press, 1985). That distinction is a special case of another, between realism and anti-realism—as fundamental a philosophical distinction as there is. On it, see John Searle, *The Construction of Social Reality* (London: Penguin, 1995), chapters 7, 8.

In effect, therefore, the question was being posed of what is *real* about being a person as such. Importantly, *is* there an inner self that could be a person? Following David Hume, §2.7 asked whether an underlying or separate inner self exists: see Hume's *A Treatise of Human Nature* (1739-40), Book I, Part IV, Section VI. On §2.8's issue of knowing oneself as a person *already* (rather than by *first* knowing one's mental states or experiences), see Strawson's *Individuals* (cited above), pp. 94-115; and Parfit's *Reasons and Persons* (Oxford: Oxford University Press, 1984), §§80-81. §2.9 applied more of the Humean thinking from §2.7: Is personal identity *over* time explicable in terms of an inner self? Or is it, more precisely, a fiction? Again see Hume's *Treatise*, Book I, Part IV, Section VI.

§2.11 considered an alternative criterion—a psychological one—of personal identity. This criterion, talking of memory (as against a persisting inner substance), comes from Locke's *Essay Concerning Human Understanding*, Book II, chapter 27. See also Parfit's *Reasons and Persons* (cited above), §§78, 83-84, 86. Fittingly, Parfit asks, too, whether identity *matters*: see §§95-96.

Then normative possibilities were discussed. On whether there is value in being a person (an issue gestured at in §2.12), see Taylor's "The Concept of a Person," in *Human Agency and Language* (above). On people being constituted by their commitments, values, and freedom (ideas discussed in §§2.14-2.17), see Jean-Paul Sartre, *Existentialism and Humanism*, trans. P. Mairet (London: Methuen, 1948). For more detailed discussion of free will (§2.17), see Robert Kane's *The Significance of Free Will* (New York: Oxford University Press, 1996).

Also, I should mention these further sources of interesting writing about many of the issues raised on Days 1 and 2 (these past two days' respective issues being tightly interwoven ones):

GENERAL (INTRODUCTORY)

Jonathan Glover, *I* (London: Penguin, 1988).

Daniel Dennett and Douglas Hofstadter (eds.), *The Mind's I* (New York: Basic Books, 1981).

John Perry (ed.), *Personal Identity* (Berkeley: University of California Press, 1975).

GENERAL (ADVANCED)

Quassim Cassam (ed.), *Self-Knowledge* (Oxford: Oxford University Press, 1994).

Raymond Martin and John Barresi (eds.), *Personal Identity* (Oxford: Blackwell, 2003).

Amelie Rorty (ed.). *The Identities of Persons* (Berkeley: University of California Press, 1976).

WHAT KIND OF THING WOULD SELF-KNOWLEDGE BE?

> In coming to understand anything we are rejecting the facts as they are for us in favour of the facts as they are. The primary impulse of each is to maintain and aggrandise himself. The secondary impulse is to go out of the self, to correct its provincialism and heal its loneliness. In love, in virtue, in the pursuit of knowledge, and in the reception of the arts, we are doing this.
>
> C.S. Lewis, *An Experiment in Criticism*

3.1 Some pessimism about knowing what self-knowledge is

Today, I'll be asking what self-knowledge actually is. First, though, I need to decide how I should even attempt to answer that question.

Maybe I could reflect upon *examples*. I would try noticing what's shared by all instances of self-knowledge—mine, anyone else's. Is that a good approach? Possibly: people often do proceed like this when seeking to understand something. For instance, if biologists want to know exactly what a whale is, in principle they examine particular whales, looking for the shared characteristics.

Wait a moment, though. That could be difficult for me to do in this case, for a few reasons.

Seemingly, the first two days showed vividly that it isn't completely obvious *what* self-knowledge I have. (Day 1: Do I know this hand as mine? That's not wholly clear. Day 2: Do I know of my having a substantial inner self, a real continuing me? This isn't obvious, either.) So, it's problematic for me to line up clear-cut *examples* of self-knowledge, so as then to ask what *makes* them instances of self-knowledge.

There is also the question of how *many* examples should be considered. No matter how many whales have been examined, we could be generalizing inaccurately: the ones we haven't examined might be quite different, in a crucial respect, to those we've seen. Surely this is also true of self-knowledge. Must I find five instances? What of six? Seven? Ten? Twenty? Where does this end? How many are enough? I don't know. I could never inspect all instances of self-knowledge; and possibly this prevents my knowing what all self-knowledge is like. (This is a problem about what's called *inductive* thinking. It's the problem of deciding what constitutes strong inductive thinking. We have to wonder when we've ever seen enough examples, enabling us to generalise appropriately.)

Here's a deeper worry. How could I know I'm examining examples of self-knowledge in the first place—unless I already know what it is? The worrying thinking behind that question, it seems, would go like this:

> I couldn't know I'm deriving (from some examples) a correct description of what self-knowledge is, if I don't already know what would make a description of self-knowledge correct. Yet to know what would make a description of self-knowledge correct, surely I must already know what self-knowledge is (so that I know the description to be accurate). So, I'll never be able to know what self-knowledge is.

I've heard of that sort of puzzle before. It's called the paradox of inquiry (or of analysis). I remember that it comes from the ancient Greek philosopher Socrates, and it challenges anyone's ever being able to understand *any* phenomenon. I've applied it here to self-knowledge; but its scope is more general. Here's how the paradox might apply to attempts to understand what it is to be a person, for instance.

(Cue two strangers, meeting under a street-light on a stormy night.)

Stranger 1: "Tell me, do, what is a person? Much depends on my knowing this!"

Stranger 2: "I think I'm one; are you, also? I can't be sure. This neighbourhood, I've heard, contains vampires, zombies, androids, and so on. Maybe we're the last two people alive. Here are photographs of two hundred other beings—all makes, all sizes. Take a look. Which ones are people (and not vampires or the like)? Observe what they have in common. Let's keep alive the concept of being a person!"

Stranger 1: "Can I know even that *I'm* a person? In order to do so, I'll *already* have to know exactly what it is to be a person. Yet I don't feel that I do; otherwise, I wouldn't be asking you about it."

Likewise, I'm puzzled. If I don't already know what self-knowledge is, surely my trying to consult supposed examples of it will be inadequate for giving me that knowledge. (And I *didn't* already know what it is. That's why I undertook this inquiry.) That's because I wouldn't know how to recognise the examples *as* instances of self-knowledge in the first place. Hence, I face the prospect of never knowing what self-knowledge is—if I would have to do so only *by* consulting examples of it to begin with. That's disturbing.

Details question. "Here I am," said the first person. "How do I know it's you? I've never met you before, and I don't know your name," replied the second person. Does that reply make sense?

3.2   *Some optimism about knowing what self-knowledge is*

Here's a more cheering thought: Stranger 1 probably knows *enough* of what it is to be a person—enough to get the inquiry moving towards knowing *more* of what it is to be a person. If that thought makes sense, perhaps the paradox of inquiry isn't wholly devastating to my chances of discovering the nature of self-knowledge (or anything else, for that matter). What *does* it show?

For a start, it shows that I cannot know *everything* there is to be known about P by examining instances of P (for any potentially widely applicable phenomenon P, such as self-knowledge, or such as being a person). Why so? The paradox amounts to the following: I don't know *all* there is to being a person, say, unless I can already know, of *every* possible being, whether it's a person; but I can't know, of *every* possible being, whether it is a person, unless I can already know *all* there is to being a person. Therefore, just inspecting examples of P (categorizing them, then generalizing from them) won't reveal the complete nature of P. So, if I have to rely on understanding examples of P, there are limits to my ability to understand P (my ability to know the nature of a phenomenon P). Should I be concerned by this limitation, implying as it does that I can never know every aspect of what self-knowledge is, for instance (this being one particular phenomenon P)?

Possibly not. In theory, there are worthwhile alternatives to total understanding. There's good understanding. There's excellent understanding. There are lots of intermediate degrees of understanding: I could understand something to *this* degree, or to *that* degree. Understanding can be better; it can be worse. I could know a lot about P without knowing everything about it; and that needn't be a problem: I could know enough about P to enable me to come to know even more about it. Maybe I know *enough* about people in that way to continue thinking in more detail about what it takes to be a person, such as when reflecting upon ethical perplexities about whether someone should remain on hospital life-support. Knowledge of what it is to be P could improve, even if it can't ever be exhaustive.

That's an optimistic thought. Still, progress in such understanding won't happen automatically, such as merely by growing older or turning up to a job. How should I proceed if I'm to sharpen my conception of self-knowledge? I don't want to rely upon random inspiration while staring at a wall. ("Insight, please. Now!") So, can I carefully, deliberately, and reflectively improve how I'm inquiring? How *should* I be inquiring if I'm to gain knowledge of what self-knowledge is? Yesterday, I noted that I was inquiring introspectively; now I'm asking how successful this (or indeed any inquiry) can be.

Well, the paradox of inquiry shows, unsurprisingly, that I cannot *begin* my inquiry by already knowing the total nature of self-knowledge or by fully knowing what makes something an instance of self-knowledge. (That's what I'm trying to find by the inquiry's end.) I have to start my intellectual trek with something in mind other than *complete* knowledge or understanding of self-knowledge. What else could there be?

That's easy. There are many options. Informed guesses—hunches and conjectures—are available. I can think of possibilities. Hypotheses can be framed. These can then be tested. How will that occur? What tests would be run? One sort of test involves expanding the hypothesised descriptions. I would fill in more and more potential details, building a larger story. My goal would be to explain ever more aspects of whatever I'm trying to understand. Then I could focus upon those details. I would ask whether they are correct, whether they provide genuine explanations. I would be asking my expanded story to be answerable to further aspects of the world, seeing if it remains coherent. If it doesn't, maybe I'll reject it entirely—discarding it as false or as not explaining what needs to be explained. Or I could sharpen, modify, and amend it, hoping to find an improved account while retaining some of it.

What might result from this theory-building, theory-modifying, and theory-testing? An understanding of self-knowledge? Not *complete* understanding: I'm unlikely ever to know *everything* about self-knowledge. Can I come to know *something* of its nature, though? There's no guarantee in advance even of that. Care—and luck—will be needed in my thinking.

Understanding question. Is it ever possible to understand something perfectly? *What* could be understood perfectly?

3.3 *Self-knowledge and other knowledge*

So, that's my broad strategy for understanding self-knowledge. How should I begin implementing it?

I mentioned informed guesses or hunches. Okay, here's one—the hypothesis that self-knowledge *is* knowledge. Although that sounds trivial, it might be quite useful.

Why so? It tells me that self-knowledge is merely one member of a more general category or kind (which we call "knowledge"), and that even if there's something distinctive about self-knowledge, maybe it isn't *wholly* distinctive. Self-knowledge could have much in common with other sorts of knowledge, including ones that seem fairly everyday. (Should that parity be surprising? No, because surely much self-knowledge would itself be everyday or mundane: my knowing I'm itchy, for instance, would be like that. Fine; but I'm wondering whether there could also be deep self-knowledge.)

Such simple thoughts allow me to think about self-knowledge indirectly, by not thinking *only* about self-knowledge. I'll think more widely, about knowledge in general. I believe I have knowledge of kangaroos, of rocks, of trees, and ... much else besides. This knowledge is of objects, animals, and the like, existing apart from me. Will this knowledge be so unlike self-knowledge that I can't learn about self-knowledge by pondering the other knowledge? I doubt it. A good zoologist learns much about animals in general before specializing (coming to know even more about kangaroos, say).

So, I'll proceed like that, by assuming there's a larger category— knowledge—within which self-knowledge is located, as a specific kind of knowledge. That's why we call self-knowledge "knowledge" in the first place. We *want* it to be knowledge, to have something in common with other kinds of knowledge. (How much in common? I don't yet know.)

This matters, because it means that I needn't treat self-knowledge as inherently mysterious, compared to other kinds of knowledge. Self-knowledge won't be a totally different kind of beast from them, so that I cannot learn about it by learning about them. On the contrary; maybe self-knowledge will *share* much of its nature with other sorts of knowledge. It mightn't be any harder to understand than other sorts of knowledge. (I don't know in advance whether this is so. I'm noting an optimistic possibility.)

That has been difficult thinking. How might I make sure of remembering its lesson?

Aha! I'll hold in mind the hypothesis that knowing myself is part of knowing the world. Self-knowledge is knowledge of the world. It is as much knowledge of the world as is knowledge of kangaroos, rocks, or trees. This is because I'm part of the world—no less real than kangaroos, rocks, and trees.

And that way of thinking coheres nicely with the hypothesis that all instances of knowledge are of aspects or parts of reality. So too, therefore, is self-knowledge; or so I'm thinking right now.

Zoological question. Can a kangaroo have self-knowledge?

3.4 Floating minds

Yet already I'm hesitant. It's tempting to say that a vital part of me—my mind—is so unlike kangaroos that knowledge of the one would be wholly unlike knowledge of the other. Lots of people might encourage me to regard my mind as being a separate kind of thing from the rest of the world. The metaphor of its "floating free" from the physical world occurs to me. Is self-knowledge therefore unique, being knowledge of something—a mind—so different in nature to the surrounding world?

That's not clear. I also feel I should resist that temptation. Sure: my mind is separate from everything else in the world. This needn't be because it's deeply separate, though, by being made of something (mental stuff?) different in kind to the physical matter comprising kangaroos. (We're continually told how much DNA we share with ... chimpanzees today, bananas the day before. No doubt, it will be kangaroos tomorrow!) Yesterday, I didn't rule out my mind's being physical. Does it occupy space within the world? "Well, it's here," I say, pointing at my head. "It's not there," I continue, pointing at the tree beside me. So, even my mind is in the world—here, not there. My mind is no less in the world than is the rock I'm kicking ... now (ouch). Each is separate from the other; neither is separate from the world as a whole. Physical or not, each is a tiny piece of the one whole.

> *Worldly question.* If a mind is not physical, how many minds can fit onto the head of a pin? How many could fit into one head?

3.5   *Deeply unique self-knowledge*

Here is another temptation I'll resist. It's the idea that no overarching theory of self-knowledge in general is possible, because each of us has unique self-knowledge. I see little merit in that idea.

Yes, my own self-knowledge would be unique in its content, in what it claims. If it wasn't, that would be odd; I *should* have knowledge about myself that no one else has. However, this needn't be because I have any miraculous *kind* of ability, possessed only by me, used when thinking about myself. No, it reflects nothing deeper than the fact that only I am me—living continually with myself, responding always to myself. No one else has a chance of knowing whether I'm feeling pain in my left leg right now; only I (if anyone) could know this. Equally, though, I have no chance of knowing whether a woman beside me in the shop is feeling pain in *her* left leg. Only she could have that knowledge; but surely she would do so in the same way as I do when knowing of my own pain. Neither of us can "get inside the other's mind"; but each of us could still be using our own mind much as the other is doing. (If my brain and hers were wired to each other, I wonder, would we merge mentally as people? Or maybe each of us would know the other's pains only as the other's pains—as "his," as "hers.")

So, it seems, my self-knowledge needn't be unique in the *kind* of thing it is. What I know about myself could be different in content, in details, to whatever others know about me or about themselves. Even so, there might be an underlying capacity or ability we share, in the midst of these differences of surface detail. The general property of having self-knowledge could be identical in everyone, even if we have unique instances of it.

Then self-knowledge would be *a single kind of state or achievement*, present around the world—common to people from varying cultures and racial ancestries. Even if everyone has their own instances of self-knowledge (thereby being somewhat different to each other), maybe we are all partly the same. What we know about ourselves would differ; the fact of our having self-knowledge at all would unite us. This would be a deep similarity between us. Even if what I know of myself is not what everyone else knows of themselves, this needn't indicate anything *deeply* unique about me. Fundamentally considered, my knowing about myself might be exactly like anyone else's knowing about themselves.

I still have to find out what self-knowledge is. The hypothesis I've offered just now can help somewhat—guiding the thinking I'm about to pursue. Here's how. If self-knowledge can be possessed around the world, by quite disparate people, there might be a basic, repeatable, core to it—one that may be described reasonably easily, in simple language. That description is what I'm seeking today. I won't assume there to be no pattern in how different people know about themselves or that my self-knowledge is unique in kind. I'll feel free to reflect upon other people, not only myself. How would others know about themselves? Intriguingly, therefore, it's possible that thinking *not* only about myself will illuminate what it would be for me to have self-knowledge.

> *Distribution question.* Might only some people have self-knowledge? Might only some people have knowledge at all?

3.6   Mere opinion

It's time to begin framing a specific hypothesis—an account, a theory—as to what self-knowledge is. Where should I begin?

I'll start with the simplest possible theory—the idea that there need not be anything in knowledge beyond *opinion*. This idea would make my inquiry extremely easy. As I sit here, thinking and writing, I would be free to regard *all* my current opinions as knowledge. Similarly for self-knowledge. Some of my current opinions are about myself; I could conclude that *all* of these are self-knowledge.

Hmm. Is that really all there is to it? Well, I do hear people talking like that about self-knowledge. All right; they'll probably concede that it isn't simply a matter of opinion as to whether I'm seeing a kangaroo, a rock, or a tree—objects in the world around me. Yet they'll say that my knowledge of what I'm like within myself is different in that respect. This is a tantalising idea: simple theories always have inherent appeal; and what I'm like in my mind, character, and main tendencies could seem to be matters on which I'm authoritative. Who's better-placed than me to know what I am like? No one! So, it's all up to me!

Seemingly, that theory would have the appeal of removing much complexity from my present investigation. At least, that would be so, if there's no deep difficulty in my deciding *what* my views are. For then (according to the suggested theory) there would be no problem in deciding what self-knowledge I have. It would be all of those easily-discovered views I have about myself. Simple?

Too simple. That way of thinking comes *too* easily to mind. For a start, I don't believe that my knowledge, even my self-knowledge, is merely a matter of my opinion. Look, we've all got opinions about ourselves, lots of them; but we have less (if any) self-knowledge. It takes no skill to have opinions, whereas knowledge usually does involve skill. I expect this to be true of self-knowledge, too. Not everything I've ever believed about myself has been knowledge. Sad, but true. How arrogant I would be to regard all my ideas about myself as knowledge. Do I know I'm intelligent, merely because I think I am? How unintelligent I would be to accept that. Am I morally insightful, simply because I believe so? How morally shallow I would be to accept that. Yesterday's musings cast doubt upon those self-serving suggestions: knowing such aspects of oneself isn't so trivial. Again sad; still true.

What's needed, then, if something is to be self-knowledge? Perhaps there are marks of real self-knowledge; and if there are, I need to find them. What does it take for one of my opinions about myself to be knowledge? (Hopefully, some of them are knowledge. Otherwise, my nature is completely hidden from me. Is that possible? Presumably so, but I'm staying optimistic.)

> *Optimism question.* Are there questions to which everyone knows the correct answer?

3.7 Self-confidence

As I glide, step, and stumble through life, in practice I use my opinions as if they're knowledge. Acting on many of them, such as when deliberating and choosing, I take them seriously as guides for thinking and moving.

At any rate, I do this except when feeling unconfident about a particular opinion. So, maybe that is part of what makes something knowledge—namely, the confidence with which it's present and used. Some opinions I hold tentatively, as ones on which I wouldn't bet much money. Do they therefore fail to be knowledge?

That's an hypothesis about knowledge in general. Applying it to self-knowledge in particular gives this proposal: Possibly, my confidence in a particular opinion about myself is the distinguishing mark of its being self-knowledge. That confidence would be a kind of *self*-confidence. It would be a confidence in how I'm seeing the world, confidence in myself as a holder of that opinion. I would be prepared to bet on that opinion about myself being true. What more could I ask of it when wondering whether it's self-knowledge?

That proposal portrays knowing as just an attitude. To know something would be to have confidence in its being so. On that proposal, a tycoon such as Donald Trump would know a lot, purely by being so confident about so much! Having confident attitudes towards the world would *be* one's knowing the world. "Gurus" and motivational speakers who exhort us to have self-confidence could (as they often do) market themselves as thereby showing us how to know ourselves.

I'm puzzled by this suggestion; but I suppose it works better as an account of knowing myself than as an account of my knowing about kangaroos. If I was so self-confident, this would "colour" all my thinking. Confidence would "take over" my mind. At which point, I would be correct in my confidence that I am confident! My confidently thinking I'm confident would be accurate. Hence, I would be knowing myself to be as my self-confidence would have *made* myself to be.

Well and good; except the issue isn't so simple. In this circumstance, that specific piece of knowledge might be my *only* one. This particular example won't allow me to generalize accurately to many, if any, other cases. Here are two related worries.

First, I would be knowing only an extremely limited aspect of myself. Sure, by being confident, I would be correct in confidently thinking I'm confident. But suppose that, although happy, I'm selfishly insensitive to others' sufferings and needs. My self-confidence, including confidence in being deeply good, could prevent my noticing this insensitivity. Most likely, I wouldn't be self-critical enough to observe this shortcoming.

Here's a more general worry. There could be much potential knowledge which self-confidence *stops* me from gaining. I've noticed this a few times in my life. Self-confidence has sometimes become careless over-confidence, which has deprived me of potential knowledge. The carelessness makes significant details less likely to be noticed. Competing interpretations of situations might also be overlooked. Admittedly, that's always possible, regardless of whether I am being overconfident at the time. Still, whenever I've been convinced already that I'm right, there has been an increased chance of paying insufficient attention to good objections against what I'm saying or thinking.

So, is self-confidence a foe of knowing? Not exactly. I don't know something if I lack all confidence in what I think about it. Knowing requires some confidence—but not too much. The same applies to self-belief: without it, one has no opinions, and I know nothing about the world if I lack all opinions about it. Knowing thus needs self-belief—but, again, not too much. Without self-confidence or self-belief, there is no self-knowledge. Yet with too much self-confidence or self-belief, sadly, there are problems for having self-knowledge.

How much self-confidence or self-belief is needed for knowledge, then? The right amount—and no more! As Goldilocks might say, "Not too little. Not too much. Just the right amount." Yes, indeed; how much *is* that?

> *Confidence question.* How much confidence is needed in knowing something? (How confident should we be in answering that question?)

3.8 Accurate confidence

Okay, so being overly confident can impede proper appreciation of what's true: not everything is whatever I confidently think it is. I'll work with this hypothesis, then: If I'm to know something, I need only as much self-confidence or self-belief as helps me to be *accurate* in thinking about that thing. Similarly for self-knowledge: in order to know some aspect of myself, I need only as much self-confidence or self-belief as will direct me towards the relevant *truth* about myself.

What that thought adds to my collection of hypotheses regarding knowledge is a claim about the relation between knowledge and accuracy. Self-knowledge involves accuracy—because any knowledge does so. If I think, even confidently, that I'm intelligent, yet I'm not, then my thought is inaccurate. It isn't knowledge, no matter how confident I am of its truth.

So I need appropriate confidence; and what is that? It is at least an accurate confidence, attuned to the right aspects of reality.

In practice, though, it's difficult ever to know that one's confidence is appropriate. The very fact of a belief's seeming to be appropriately confident can itself function as over-confidence! Because it seems true, one could relax into assuming it's true. Even when mistaken in a belief, I could easily overlook this, fooled by the belief's seeming true.

Here's an example. Suppose I confidently believe that whales are fish. It's a mistaken belief; but try telling me that! I might admit that maybe I'm wrong; yet perhaps I'm accepting this possibility only in a patronizing or detached way. In contrast, if I were to begin understanding how, really, I might be wrong ("Aha! I was misunderstanding basic biology"), that should also weaken my confidence that whales are fish. Until then, I remain confident, because I don't genuinely see why I shouldn't. ("What? Me mistaken? But I seem so right!") Equally, while ever I maintain my confidence, I'm not genuinely seeing why I shouldn't.

Yes, it can happen that afterwards—when, for whatever reason, I no longer have that confident belief about whales—I'll decide that my previous belief wasn't true. Only then, only afterwards, will I have the psychological "distance" enabling me to think of myself as having been mistaken. So, there's a trap built into how I negotiate the world with my opinions. While still "in the grip" of a belief (holding it confidently),

I cannot decide that, really, it's false. Nor can I honestly comprehend why it should be discarded as false. I have the confidence because I think I should; by having it, I don't see that I shouldn't.

In theory, I might admit that my belief could be false (and that, at some later time, it may well be discarded as false). Right now, though, I can't do that; and, in practice, will this lead to my treating the belief as if it could not be false? Maybe so. Yet this is a trap. I shouldn't be that impressed by my own confidence. Being somewhat confident is part of *having* a belief; it needn't be part of the belief's being *true*. (Even trying to correct my thoughts immediately after having them won't escape this problem. Thinking back now, upon thoughts I've had as recently as a minute ago, I could be mistaken at this very moment in assessing them.) Even if I know I've made mistakes in the past, can I know I'm making a mistake now, in holding a particular belief? No way. If I could, I wouldn't still *have* the belief. I can evaluate the belief properly only when I don't have it—or at least only once I'm no longer holding it confidently. (Is it possible to have weaker beliefs, ones allowing for their potentially being mistaken? I'm not sure. For now, at least, I'll continue focussing upon unequivocally confident beliefs or opinions.)

There are many ways in which this failing characterises people's lives. For instance, I'm often struck by how readily we acknowledge that the best artists haven't always been recognised as such during their lifetimes, when still working. We also accept that many minor talents, lauded while alive, are now devalued, usually rightly so. We realize this, even as we cannot imagine how those artists we regard as the best now are not actually so amazing. Maybe the current favourites will be scorned, and rightly so, by later generations. Nonetheless, we might be unable to see *how* the current favourites could be rightly spurned. If we *were* to see this, we would have to cease thinking of these favourites so favourably; then where would we be? (Yes, we might be able, one of these days, to replace our commitment to them with a commitment to others. That won't escape the basic problem—which simply recurs, applying to our new commitment.) Every era finds and rewards its "stars." Yet maybe not all eras produce people of real talent. Might our own era be a time of genuinely bad taste in the art most praised by modern art galleries and critics? Possibly, this is a period when no one of significant and lasting talent is alive. (Similarly, perhaps no philosopher alive today will be remembered, let alone respected, 100 years hence.) However, a vast number of people seem unable to accommodate this idea within their reactions to actual individual artists. ("His work will live forever," said of someone whose paintings have been well-regarded, even popular, for 20 years. Surely such praise is premature. "Her vision is so timeless," remarked of work that could well turn out to be, like much that has gone before, a passing fad.)

The problem is widespread within human thinking. People regularly say things like, "We're all fallible; we all make mistakes." This sounds pleasingly humble. Do people often take that lesson into their heart, becoming genuinely humble in their thinking? It's hard—is it impossible?—really to accept that a belief one confidently has could be mistaken. Because I can't see a belief as mistaken while still having it confidently, in practice I treat it—while I have it—as if it cannot be mistaken.

This might help to explain the popular tendency to assume that being confident in an opinion is enough to make it knowledge. It's tempting to think that when an opinion cannot be mistaken, it's knowledge; and, as I've seen just now, whenever I have an opinion confidently, I cannot maintain my confidence in it while simultaneously seeing how it really could be wrong. Sure, I'll say, "Admittedly I could be mistaken"; but I do so without really *feeling* that it might be mistaken. It feels to me like knowledge.

Again, though, that's a trick my mind plays upon me. Being confident in a belief's truth is necessary to holding the belief (which is one's holding it as true). Nevertheless, none of this guarantees the belief's *being* true. Confidence doesn't guarantee accuracy or, therefore, knowledge. ("What's the alternative? Should we become pessimists?" I hope not. I'll try to return to this fundamental question later, although maybe—I don't yet know—I won't have time for it today.)

> *Accuracy question.* Is it more accurate to say that murder is very immoral than simply to call it immoral?

3.9 Luck

Still, sometimes I *am* both confident and accurate in my thinking. Are these occasions of knowing something? Maybe self-knowledge is present whenever an opinion I have about myself is both confident and accurate. Okay, rarely does being confident guarantee accuracy. Whenever those two qualities *are* conjoined, though, perhaps this amounts to having a piece of knowledge. For instance, if I confidently (although not overconfidently) think I have a hand, and if I'm right, do I thereby know that I have one?

Unfortunately, I've already seen (on Day 1) why it might not be simple for me to know that a hand I'm seeing is mine; and I haven't yet evaded those difficulties. Even so, I'm still confident (in a normal-but-not-particularly-philosophical way) of the hand I see here ... this one ... being mine; and what I'm confident of could well be accurate. Rationally speaking, however, a question remains as to whether I should have that confidence. Right now, I'm not sure—because I haven't yet overthrown those earlier worries—whether I know the hand to be mine. Possibly, this is a case of lacking knowledge even while being both confident and correct.

How could that be so? Simple: being both confident and correct could be a coincidence. Confidence may arise in different ways, not all of which are sensitive to truth. My confidence might have only luckily been associated with my accepting something that, as it happens, is true. But truth—accuracy—is essential to knowing. Must I have a good link to a truth, then, if I'm to know it? It's natural to think that I lack knowledge whenever there's only an *accidental* or *lucky* pairing of confidence and accuracy.

I'll test that idea. I feel confident that it's just after 2 p.m. What gives me this confidence? A moment ago, after walking out of my office, I looked at the clock on the corridor wall. The clock indicated the time as 2 o'clock. "Fine. It's 2 p.m.," I thought. Back to my office; I began writing this paragraph. It *is* now slightly after 2 p.m. But let's suppose that—without my realizing it—the clock was broken. I'll imagine that it had stopped with its hands showing 2 o'clock. It would therefore be correct twice each day—at 2 a.m. and 2 p.m. By chance, I saw it at—yes, indeed—2 p.m. What I'm confident of is therefore accurate. Is it also knowledge? Do I *know* that the time is just after 2 p.m.? I might well feel as if I do. Perhaps I don't really know, though; I'm just lucky in being accurate this time.

It's quite possible then, that confidence-plus-accuracy isn't enough, on its own, for knowledge.

> *Luck question.* If I cannot tell the difference between a toad and a frog, am I wrong when saying, while pointing at a frog, "I know that's a frog"?

3.10   Normal circumstances

What *is* enough for knowledge? I'll think further about the example of the stopped clock. It might provide clues as to the nature of knowledge.

When glancing at the clock, I treated it as working normally. I took for granted the situation's relevant normality. This helped to generate my confidence, because I didn't realize that my assumption was false: the situation wasn't normal. Due to that falsity, moreover, I was lucky to form a confident belief (in its being just after 2 p.m.) which was true. When building upon what's mistaken, further mistakes become more likely. Falsity begets falsity! (Lie once; further lies are needed, if only to cover up the initial lie. Adopt one mistaken idea; presumably, additional mistakes become more likely.)

I wasn't consciously assuming the situation's normality. Everything happened quickly. Glancing up, I registered the time, then looked away—all in an instant. Still, I guess that an assumption needn't consciously be used. It could be silent, unnoticed at the time.

Fair enough; what's the moral of those thoughts? I assumed that the adjacent world was operating normally and that I was reacting to it normally. By being mistaken in part of that assumption, I failed to gain knowledge. Even so, where exactly was the main fault? Maybe it was the circumstance's not *being* normal. Alternatively, it could have been my being mistaken in *assuming* its being normal. The former failing would be the more fundamental of those two, I suppose. After all, correcting it will probably *include* correcting the latter: normality in my circumstances includes my assuming there to be normality in my circumstances! (Making that assumption is part of how I normally think. It's something the world normally encourages me to think.)

Consequently, perhaps knowledge is present only in normal circumstances. Whenever I'm in such circumstances, it seems, an accurate confidence is all I need if I'm to know something. If everything in a circumstance is functioning normally, then knowing an aspect of the world is just a matter of being right in what one thinks, in the circumstance. In saying this, however, I mustn't undervalue or forget the contribution of that normality—that surrounding or underlying circumstance of normality. Thus, I have this new hypothesis: Knowledge is an accurate confidence, present as part of a normal circumstance. Yes?

Normality question. Can normality be defined?

3.11 Reliability

If I'm to decide whether that's what knowledge is, details are needed. In particular, what is it for circumstances to be normal?

Presumably, normal circumstances involve a kind of causal stability (in other words, an underlying pattern of regularity, being "well ordered" and structured by laws of nature). I believe this is required if the world is to be knowable at all—if it's to be something that *could* be known, the right kind of thing *ever* to be known. In order to test that belief, I'll try imagining the world's *lacking* such stability.... Hmm. I'm not sure I can. It's hard, maybe impossible, to imagine the details of such a world—precisely *because* it's unstable. That world would be continually surprising, too much so to be knowable, it seems to me. If I was living in that world, I couldn't develop or learn dependable patterns of behaviour—ways of fitting in with, and responding to, how the world was functioning—on the basis of what I would have observed. There would be a kind of chaos, impeding all predictability. Today, the sun would have risen; tomorrow, it might well not do so; yesterday, maybe, it didn't. Today, pears would taste different from mangoes; tomorrow, maybe they won't. On and on it would go: the possibilities are endless; no changes would be foreseeable. That wouldn't be a knowable world.

I wouldn't even know what to call anything in the first place, if this world was like that! Would this piece of fruit even *be* a pear, given what would happen to it? Would it even *be* fruit, given how it would (mis)behave? Would it even *be* a physical thing, given such oddities? (And everyone within that world would act so haphazardly, erratically. Within such a setting, won't I fail to know who, even what, they are?)

Thus, a world's having an underlying sort of stability is needed, if it's to be a world that allows us to know or understand it. If we know this world of ours reasonably well, in part that's *because* it's basically stable. (As far as we can tell, it has natural laws, ones which science has a chance of uncovering.)

That need for stability (if knowledge is to be present) also applies to *me*, as someone living and functioning within this world: I know aspects of the world, only if *I'm* stable in relevant ways. The world's stability must encompass my senses—how they're working, what they're telling me. It must also cover my reasoning—how I sort and evaluate whatever apparent information reaches me. In short, it has to support however I form and maintain beliefs. My observing and thinking must be causally stable. Random observational or mental fits and starts won't be much help in revealing the world's nature to me. Attending only poorly to how the stable, well-ordered, world around me is functioning wouldn't be a way of knowing the world. I mustn't be responding to the world as if I'm "in my own mental world."

Aha. There's a stable pattern to those thoughts about stability. They seem to imply that my knowing something includes my reacting in a causally stable way to an aspect of a causally stable world. This would be a sort of *fit* or *harmony* between me (observing and reasoning stably) and the stable world. Is this the key to my knowing the world? I must be *linked* like that to the world ("in tune with it"), if I'm to have knowledge of it.

That would be a sort of *reliability* as a thinker. When someone is reliable, they're dependable. If they say they'll meet you at 10 a.m. by the entrance to the park, they do so, unless something unusual prevents it. A reliable thinker is like that, too. If I'm reliably confident about something, this confidence is accurate, unless something untoward intervenes. In most settings, reliability doesn't have to be perfect; it need only be good. Is that what knowing requires, then—a very (even if not perfectly) reliable confidence?

If so, then knowledge is a confidence which *is* accurate, and which arose in a way that made it *very likely* to be accurate. According to such an hypothesis, if I know it's 3 p.m. when looking at my watch, that's because I'm confident and correct in thinking that it is now 3 p.m., *and* because looking at my watch is a reliable way of forming accurate beliefs about what time it is.

> *Reliability question.* How much of a person's being brilliant is his or her being reliable?

3.12 Good evidence

Sometimes, I'm asked to explain or justify my opinions. (How puzzling it is that not everyone believes everything I say, with no questions asked!) Actually, I even subject myself to such testing. When contemplating something complicated, such as conflicting ideas between which I must choose, it's of little use to think like this:

> I'm confident of ... this idea ... (not that other one ...); but do I know it's true? I'm assuming that I have the idea in a normal way. If that assumption is true, then—so long as the idea, too, is accurate—the idea is knowledge. (An example: "Is there a God? I believe so; and I assume that my belief in God's existing has arisen normally—such as via religious upbringing. So, if my belief is accurate, it's knowledge.")

I realize that such reasoning doesn't determine whether the idea *is* knowledge. It merely presents reasoning for why the idea might be knowledge— why it's knowledge *if* various conditions are satisfied. If I defended my opinions only in that way, I should be deemed either stupid or dogmatic.

How may that unhelpful approach be avoided? It seems that *evidence* should be sought whenever this is feasible and potentially useful. No, even this isn't enough; *good* evidence should be sought. I've often heard people offering evidence that is clearly self-serving, incomplete, biased, and so on. This process is easily abused. ("I have evidence for what I'm saying. So you can't dismiss my view. It's *my* position.") This isn't a way to gain knowledge—real knowledge.

What makes evidence genuinely good? I use the word "genuinely" to designate evidence which actually is good, rather than merely seeming to be good. In practice, it can be difficult to know whether some particular evidence *is* actually good. This difficulty, however, doesn't imply that there is *no* actually good, or actually bad, evidence. Depressingly many people offer what they claim is good evidence, when really they are voicing rationalizations—convenient excuses for not questioning some favoured view or self-serving action, excuses masquerading as impartial reasons for adopting that view or for approving of that action. Maybe we're all subject to this failing some of the time. But I've known a few people for whom it's habitual. When in the grip of a political or emotional idea, for example, some people are bad at reacting impartially and fair-mindedly to evidence, or at searching assiduously and open-mindedly for evidence (happy to follow wherever it leads, willing to learn whatever it might reveal).

What's *wrong* with not being impartial, fair-minded, assiduous, open-minded, and the like, in how one approaches evidence? One failing is evident: such people are less *reliable* as guides to what is true. They are more likely to notice only what they want to notice. They overlook more of what shouldn't be overlooked when truth is needed. In short, because people who use evidence poorly are less reliable guides to what is true, they don't *know* as much as they think they do.

I would rather not be like that. Reliability is needed, I'll accept, in how opinions are formed or maintained, if they're to be knowledge; and using good evidence is a way for reliability to be present. Good evidence is evidence which makes some belief or confidence very likely to be true. Even if I form or defend a belief by citing evidence I think supports it, that won't make the belief knowledge if the evidence doesn't *actually* make the belief very likely to be true. Is this sort of reliability therefore the point of having actually good evidence? I think it's part of the point.

Evidence question. What are some differences between good and bad evidence?

3.13 Agreeing with other people

How do other people's opinions feature in all this? I'm wondering, because other people and their opinions contribute significantly to the normality of many situations.

For example, if (as I'm conjecturing) an opinion is knowledge only so long as the circumstances of gaining or keeping it are normal, must this include other people agreeing with it? Maybe knowing something requires fitting in with how others think about it. Then again, even if agreement with others isn't required, perhaps it is sufficient. Is any opinion knowledge once it accords with what others think? It's socially normal to agree generally with other people, believing them, deferring to many, and so on. It's abnormal, in that sense, to have unusual opinions. Possibly, therefore, agreeing with others is part of knowing.

I've been told by several people that knowledge is social ("It's socially constituted"), in that what makes something knowledge is its being what most of us believe, within an entire society or some smaller group. Is that hypothesis about knowledge accurate? Do I know there is a god, for instance, if everyone around me says that we know there to be one? That's an unrealistic case, because inevitably disagreements exist: rarely does everyone in a community think there is a god. All right, then, maybe I would know that there's a god, simply by being among a *majority* of people who believe there to be one.

No, I doubt that agreement with others has such decisiveness in gaining truth and knowledge. It wouldn't be an *ultimate* part of what makes something knowledge (rather than merely a confident opinion). Other people can be mistaken, just like me. Why should their opinions be inherently decisive, if mine isn't? Groups of people can go wrong, too—reinforcing mistakes, oversights, or narrow thinking among themselves. Often I've been misled by others; I'll bet they've been similarly misled at times. I'm not advocating always ignoring other opinions. That would be foolish: they could have much valuable knowledge to impart. (So, maybe I should return to this topic tomorrow.) Nonetheless, all of us, as individuals and in groups, can make mistakes. (There was a time when, inaccurately, people in general believed the earth to be flat. These days, still inaccurately, some individuals maintain that belief.) Knowing is ultimately about fitting in with the wider world, not only with others around us. Accepting what I'm told by others—parents, neighbours, teachers, and so forth—gives me knowledge only when they already have it to give.

So, that "wholly social" way of trying to understand knowledge's presence won't take me far in itself. On the current suggestion, those other people also have knowledge only socially, when accepting what further people have told them. Fine; but the further people, too, need to be imparting knowledge *they* possess. How would they have it? Presumably (again on the current proposal), by accepting knowledge from other people. Again fine; but how would these other people have this knowledge? By agreeing with still more people? This sort of explanation cannot continue forever: there's a limit to how many people may have knowledge courtesy of others. (The supply of people gives out!)

This suggestion is really saying that knowledge is whatever some *tradition* accepts; and lots of people are willing to live in subservience to traditions of thought. However, traditions mightn't always be storehouses of knowledge. Traditions impart knowledge only if either they begin with knowledge or, independently, they develop knowledge along the way; which won't always happen. Our forebears were real people, with fallibilities and failings as strong and real as ours. They weren't superheroes with super-minds. They needed to be genuinely reliable in their thinking (not just regarding each other as reliable), if they were to be founts of knowledge. They mightn't have *been* reliable, though, on a given topic or claim.

Accordingly, agreeing with others is never all there is to something's being knowledge. It's possible for agreement with others to *transmit* knowledge without *constituting* it. The agreement can also transmit beliefs which people *mistakenly* think are knowledge. When accepting what others say, I may be gaining beliefs which aren't knowledge. Even when I'm gaining knowledge from others, agreeing with them needn't be what *makes* the belief I'm gaining knowledge. Agreeing can spread knowledge without making something knowledge in the first place.

Of course, the fact that others accept a particular belief is some evidence in its favour: if they accept it, maybe it's true. This evidence can, but needn't, then help to make the belief knowledge.

A group of people can also "construct" some knowledge by collectively developing an answer to a question or problem. Scientists typically seek knowledge in this way; but any answer they derive isn't knowledge simply because it's their shared opinion or even because they agree on its being knowledge. It's knowledge only if they've collectively been accurate and reliable. The point, as I see it, is that agreeing with others isn't enough to make a belief knowledge. (Nor is it always needed. Evidence can take forms other than agreement among people.) What matters most, I suppose, is agreeing with the right people—accurate and reliable ones. That could be knowledge. Agreeing with *just more* people isn't enough.

Yet in practice how do I know who are the right people? This isn't always decided both socially and accurately. If someone, even an "official" expert, isn't correct, I don't gain knowledge by accepting what he or she says. If the "expert" isn't reliable, the official evidence being offered mightn't be very good. Admittedly, in practice I probably have no independent way of knowing whether "experts" I'm hearing are reliable. (Students, I gather, often judge teachers' competence by such irrelevant criteria as stylish or "authoritative" clothes, an air of confidence, even gender.) In practice, I must trust official, socially appointed, experts—hearing them on the radio and TV, listening to them at university, reading them in newspapers and elsewhere. Nevertheless, that practical need to treat official experts' claims as knowledge doesn't imply that whatever they tell me *is* knowledge. Hopefully, it usually is; regrettably, it won't always be.

Experts question. Are there experts on being an expert? (Could they disagree with each other?)

3.14 Unusual knowledge

That's both heartening and worrying. The worry is obvious; and there's not much I can do about it, apart from being intellectually vigilant and not accepting uncritically everything I'm told (even by official experts). I'll concentrate now on the cheerier aspect of what I've been thinking— which is that, even in requiring knowledge to reflect an accurate sense of normality, I'm not ruling out the possibility of knowing something unusual or of knowing something in an unusual way (a way no one else notices). Knowing something needn't involve agreeing with others, I've found. Being socially odd in having a particular thought doesn't prevent its being knowledge. It could be knowledge even if others don't agree.

So, the sort of oddity which, I've been thinking, hinders an opinion's being knowledge is causal, not social. For example, when looking at the clock gave me a correct belief about the time, although the clock was stopped, this was relevantly odd because looking at a stopped clock rarely causes a correct belief as to what time it is (and because a clock being looked at is rarely stopped). I was lucky! That's why, it seems, I didn't gain knowledge (even though I gained an accurate belief) as to its being shortly after 2 p.m.

Occasionally, I've woken up in the morning, feeling that in the middle of the night, during a dream, I had solved a deep philosophical puzzle. Naturally, I never remember the details. Once or twice, I've tried getting out of bed during the night, writing down thoughts without fully waking up. In the morning, I reached for the paper on which I had written ... gibberish! Oh well. Still, I live in hope. There might be a morning when I'll remember my dreamt philosophical thoughts and they'll be significant. Could I thereby have gained knowledge in my dreams? ("Only in your dreams," someone will reply, dismissively.)

I suspect it isn't possible. Presumably, the way in which I would have gained the confidence *is* odd in the relevant sense—the causal sense. The world doesn't proceed in that way, revealing itself for the first time in people's dreams. In which case, I won't have woken up with fresh philosophical knowledge. (What of self-knowledge? Might it be found in dreams? Memo to self: think about this tomorrow!) The lack of knowledge wouldn't be because people deride dreams as not giving knowledge. (If, as I found, agreement with others isn't enough to make an opinion knowledge, disagreement with others isn't enough to prevent an opinion's being knowledge. I might have knowledge no one else has. Thinking like everyone else isn't always needed for having a particular piece of knowledge.) No, the failing would be more objective. It would be a *fact* about how the world of cause-and-effect works. That's why the dream wouldn't give me knowledge. The problem is that dreams are not reliably good guides to what is true, to how the world really is.

Sometimes, I admit, something that isn't knowledge could reliably give rise to knowledge. For instance, inspired by an interesting idea in my dream, I might continue reflecting upon that idea until I accumulate good evidence supporting it. Would this turn my initially unreliable confidence into knowledge? People often think they must have known *all along*, once they discover that they were right about something. (Perhaps this is part of people's readiness to believe that a psychic knew from the outset, whenever one of his or her confident predictions is found to be true.) Yet it's possible to start out being right about something without knowing it—and only later, maybe after gaining good evidence one formerly lacked, to find oneself knowing it. I could dream a philosophical insight, a philosophical truth—only later, after effort and inquiry, transforming that correct opinion into knowledge. The dream provided the initial idea; subsequent philosophical work was needed, if the idea was to become real philosophical knowledge. I would have found good evidence in favour of the idea, rendering my acceptance of it far more likely to be true—with it only now being reliably believed.

Even then, the knowledge could be socially odd (such as if the evidence I find isn't widely accepted). This might be society's loss, though. The evidence could be genuinely good anyway, in spite of other people not recognizing how good it is. Maybe they'll even dismiss the person (who, I'm imagining, is me!—gasp, sob) as a crackpot, as "out of touch." Of course, many people who advocate ideas, and who use evidence, rejected by others are indeed crackpots. They can be far from having the knowledge they claim to have. Nonetheless, I won't rudely dismiss someone simply because he or she is thinking oddly. (Surely some areas of thought, philosophy among them, should be especially open to unusual ideas, to the imagination. That's part of what made philosophy attractive to me in the first place when I was 17. It still does.) A person could have knowledge by responding accurately and reliably to an aspect of the world, even if he or she is the only person who has noticed this aspect or who is thinking in this unusual (although reliable) way. I don't see why there cannot be some knowledge which is surprising—and rarely possessed—in that way. (Sometimes, others later come to see the world in that same way, agreeing with the person whose views had previously seemed so odd. A scientific or philosophical breakthrough might be like this.)

What does this tell me? For a start: Don't assume that majority opinions are always right.

Unusual question. What might be the oddest way in which someone has ever known something?

3.15 Self-knowledge

I think I've made some progress today, by isolating key features of what, in general, it is to know something. Now I'll begin applying that general account of knowledge to self-knowledge in particular.

The picture will be that self-knowledge is a kind of self-confidence. Not just any self-confidence will do, though—because accuracy and reliability are needed (more so than uplifting optimism, for instance). Self-knowledge needn't make me feel good about myself. I'm confident that I should not be confident about various of my abilities being especially good! An accurate confidence—based on reliably good evidence of what I'm like—might give me little optimism about some of my abilities. It needn't be a belief that I possess deeply developed skills. It might reveal my having normal abilities, nothing extraordinary. Why couldn't "I'm normal, nothing special" be self-knowledge? It could; in my case, it is!

Is self-knowledge thereby unimportant? Far from it. If I'm to have self-belief that isn't mere vanity, it had better be based on self-knowledge. Any fool is able to spin fantasies about what he or she can do: I may believe for the rest of my life that I could have become an international sports star—so long as I conveniently forget that my reflexes were not sufficiently quick, my power was inadequate, my desire to play cricket to the exclusion of all else wasn't strong enough, and the like. That list is oh-so-long. Any related self-knowledge I have should respect it.

> *Revealing question.* What *should* people most want to know about themselves? What, it seems, *do* people most want to know about themselves?

3.16   Where to next?

Is self-knowledge difficult to gain? Today's reflections convince me that there can be more to having it than I had anticipated. Maybe that's why Days 1 and 2 found me struggling to know myself. I encountered potential problems about knowing either my physical self or my mental self. Today, I appreciate better why that knowledge isn't trivially attainable. Self-knowledge is not mere self-belief; it's present only when comparatively stringent standards are met.

Are there methods for meeting such standards? How might I best try to satisfy today's account of self-knowledge—possibly so as to gain, more methodically, all or some of the self-knowledge I sought on those earlier two days? Tomorrow, I'll set out to answer that question.

> *Awkward question.* What *should* people least want to know about themselves? What, it seems, *do* people least want to know about themselves?

3.17 Overview of the day

This difficult day's thinking has focussed on this basic question: What is self-knowledge? I proposed various hypotheses, including these:

> Knowledge is accurate confidence (occurring normally, not too oddly) about some aspect of the world.

That normality makes the confidence reliably accurate. (Using good evidence contributes to that reliability.) So, knowledge is a reliably accurate confidence. (For example, it's a belief that is true and was also likely to be true, given how it was formed or how it is being supported.)

Self-knowledge is knowledge, as characterised above, of aspects of oneself.

Then extra questions arise, such as these ones:

> Could only people have self-knowledge? When a chimpanzee studies a reflection of itself in a mirror, is the animal studying its self as such? When people look at reflections of themselves in a mirror, are they gazing upon their selves as such? Is knowing an acquired ca-

pacity? (If so, how would it be acquired? By normal physical development? By some forms of social development?) When do babies or young children begin using knowledge? How do we know it's knowledge—rather than almost-knowledge, or something similar—that they have? (When can we be deceived in attributing knowledge to others?) Do people ever cease developing as knowers? Do some people make lots of mistakes—even the same ones, over and over—in ordinary observing and thinking? Does this somehow restrict or stunt their personhood? (Could philosophy help us to avoid this?)

FURTHER READING

Today's musing began, in §3.1, with a challenge as to whether philosophical knowledge is ever possible. (Days 1 and 2 sought philosophical knowledge of the self.) On the paradox of inquiry, see Roy Sorensen's *A Brief History of the Paradox* (New York: Oxford University Press, 2003), chapters 5, 6.

§3.2 suggested a way of proceeding, nonetheless. Hypotheses and informed hunches were to lead the way, with reflective examination following: we may call this theory-building. On such notions, see W.V. Quine and J.S. Ullian, *The Web of Belief* (New York: Random House, 1970), chapters V, VII, and VIII. For more on the conceptual difficulty in this, see Roderick Chisholm's *Theory of Knowledge*, 3rd edition (Englewood Cliffs, NJ: Prentice Hall, 1989), chapter 1.

Theorizing therefore began, next buttressed by the suggestion (§§3.3-3.5) that philosophical theorizing about knowledge in general may apply to self-knowledge in particular. For an influential argument to this effect, see Gilbert Ryle's *The Concept of Mind* (Harmondsworth, UK: Penguin, 1963), chapter VI, section (4). What, then, *is* knowledge in general?

Might knowledge be, as §§3.6-3.7 hypothesised, an *opinion* (or *belief*—this being the term most commonly used among philosophers)? Almost all philosophers believe knowledge to be some sort of belief or opinion. See, for example, Laurence BonJour, *Epistemology* (Lanham, MD: Rowman & Littlefield, 2002), pp. 27-32. For a prominent argument against knowledge's being any kind of belief at all, see Plato's *Republic*, Book V (475b-480).

Still, even if knowledge is an opinion, might additional features be needed? §3.8 asked whether knowledge is merely an *accurate* opinion (or *true* belief—again to use the usual term). Crispin Sartwell argues for knowledge's being like that: "Why Knowledge is Merely True Belief," *The Journal of Philosophy* 89 (1992), 167-80. In contrast, most philosophers *deny* that knowledge is simply an accurate opinion. (They rely upon thought-experiments like §3.9's, concerning the stopped clock. It is from Bertrand Russell's *Human Knowledge* (London: George Allen and Unwin, 1948), pp. 170-1.) The classic source for that denial is Plato's dialogue, *Meno* (96e-100b).

Which additional features would be needed within knowledge, though? A few possibilities were presented here. §3.10 stressed the relevance of *normal* circumstances. For a related theory of knowledge (also conceiving of knowledge in terms of functioning properly within an appropriate environment), see Alvin Plantinga's *Warrant and Proper Function* (New York: Oxford University Press, 1993). §3.11 considered whether these normal circumstances must be causally stable, including there being a kind of *reliability* in one's thinking. On ancient Greek philosophers' first formulating a concept of the world's causal stability, see Gregory Vlastos, *Plato's Universe* (Seattle: University of Washington Press, 1978). On reliability in one's thinking, see Alvin Goldman's "What is Justified Belief?", in George Pappas (ed.), *Justification and Knowledge* (Dordrecht, Holland: Reidel, 1979). §3.12 argued for the normal circumstances needing to involve *good evidence*. On this potential need, see Earl Conee and Richard Feldman, "Evidentialism," in their book *Evidentialism* (Oxford: Oxford University Press, 2004).

The resulting theory is standardly known as the *justified true belief* theory of knowledge; I'll call it the *well-supported accurate opinion* theory of knowledge. Versions of it were first discussed—critically—by Plato, in his *Theaetetus* (201c-210d); for analysis, see F.M. Cornford, *Plato's Theory of Knowledge* (London: Routledge & Kegan Paul, 1935), pp. 142-63. There are many contemporary philosophical expositions—and discussions—of this form of theory. See, for example, A.J. Ayer, *The Problem of Knowledge* (London: Macmillan, 1956), chapter 1; Stephen Hetherington, *Knowledge Puzzles* (Boulder, CO: Westview Press, 1996), chapters 2-11; Adam Morton, *A Guide Through the Theory of Knowledge*, 3rd edition (Oxford: Blackwell, 2003), chapter 6; Paul Moser, *Knowledge and Evidence* (Cambridge: Cambridge University Press, 1989), chapter 1.

Today has ended (§3.13) with the question of whether knowing (its normality, its reliability, its use of good evidence) must include—or even be wholly constituted by—agreement with other people. For cautious comment, see Quine and Ullian, *The Web of Belief* (cited above), chapter IV. For a spirited sally, see Alvin Goldman's *Knowledge in a Social World* (Oxford: Oxford University Press, 1999), chapter 1.

DAY 4 | HOW MIGHT SELF-KNOWLEDGE BE GAINED?

> The man who is contented to be only himself, and therefore less
> a self, is in prison. My own eyes are not enough for me.... [I]n
> reading great literature I become a thousand men yet remain
> myself. Like the night sky in the Greek poem, I see with a myriad
> eyes, but it is still I who see. Here, as in worship, in love, in moral
> action, and in knowing, I transcend myself; and am never more
> myself than when I do.
>
> C.S. Lewis, *An Experiment in Criticism*

4.1   Methods? Which methods?

Yesterday, a general picture of knowledge unfolded; and I'd like to hold
that picture in mind. One handy motto or shorthand for it would be this:
To know something is to have a well-supported and accurate opinion.
So, I speak of a *well-supported accurate opinion* conception of knowledge.
(I've also heard this called a *justified-true-belief* conception.)

I went to sleep, expecting that self-knowledge will satisfy that account of knowledge in general: self-knowledge is like any other kind of
knowledge, in being a well-supported and accurate opinion. (It's just
that the opinions are about oneself.) Okay; so today I'll ask *how* I might

gain such self-knowledge (assuming, for now, that this is possible). Are there special methods for obtaining it?

Yesterday's thoughts imply that these methods would be reliable ways of forming or defending accurate opinions about myself; and the methods could include apt uses of good evidence (making the accurate opinions well-supported). By using such methods, I might gain self-knowledge; without them, I won't (because at best I would have accurate but not well-supported opinions). So, it's clear that when claiming self-knowledge I need to think about *how* I form and defend my opinions, my beliefs, about myself. *Am* I generally using reliable methods on those occasions?

I used to assume so. Now that I'm thinking more critically, I'm less sure. So much so that, suddenly, I'm not even certain that it's ever obvious *what* method I'm using.

When looking at this hand, for example, in which specific way am I reaching the belief that it's mine? The everyday answer is that I'm seeing the hand as mine. However, "seeing" denotes a broad category. I could equally well have said that I'm seeing the hand today, or seeing it this week, or seeing it while thinking critically, or seeing it while being puzzled by philosophical questions about self-knowledge, and so on. Which one of these am I using? These can be called different possible specific methods; and *each* description, seemingly, is applying to me. Yet surely these different methods aren't *equally* reliable; and maybe not each is reliable *enough* to be giving me knowledge. So there's urgency in asking, "Which, exactly, is being used?" It's arbitrary to single out just one of them. Nonetheless, surely this must be done, if I'm to say definitively that (by using a specific method) I know this to be my hand. (Otherwise, *how* have I ended up with the belief that this is my hand? Do I not know?)

I'm tempted to reply that my method is that of using my eyes *exactly now*, in these *completely specific* circumstances, to decide whether this is my hand. But this reply wouldn't describe a method as such. Anything that's a method can, in theory, be re-used (compiling a "track record" of some degree of reliability). Yet no wholly specific circumstance could ever reappear. This circumstance of using my eyes exactly ... now ... is gone forever, as ... now ... I'm using my eyes in a new circumstance ... which itself is ... now ... gone forever, as ... now ... I'm using my eyes in a new circumstance. On and on this could continue, one new circumstance succeeding another, none repeated: "now, now, very now" (as Iago says in Shakespeare's *Othello*). Hence, no two of my opinions (even when sharing their content, such as "This is my hand") would ever arise via the same method. (By arising in their respective unique circumstances, each would be generated in a completely new way.) Yesterday, though, I decided that knowing is not only being right; it's being right in a way that, at least in theory, can be maintained or repeated. Knowing is partly methodological; being right needn't be (because it could be quite fluky or accidental). Whenever I know something, this is due partly to my using *some* method (even if not consciously).

Still, even if I *am* using a method when forming (or, for that matter, defending) a particular belief, it's not clear that I ever *know* for sure which one I'm using. Perhaps I'm left, therefore, never knowing exactly how I'm forming an opinion? I would never know for sure whether I'm forming a belief reliably; and so I won't know for sure whether my belief is knowledge. Where does this leave me? Should I *discard* my optimistic assumption that sometimes I have knowledge?

> *Counting question.* I'm sitting in a chair. I'm also in a room. How many circumstances am I in? Just those two? Could the actual number be limitless?

4.2 Intuition

No, I won't yet discard that optimistic assumption (of my sometimes having knowledge). Instead, I'll think about whether it is possible to know something without knowing exactly *how* this knowledge has arisen. Could self-knowledge, especially, be like that? In asking this, I'm wondering whether *intuition* can be a source of knowledge, particularly self-knowledge.

People often use the term "intuition" to designate a way of knowing which they believe can't be understood. Any intuitive self-knowledge would be present inexplicably, not open to further analysis or understanding; and many people are receptive to the idea that much self-knowledge is like this. If I ask such people how they know their inner characters, I'm likely to be told that they have "an intuitive sense" of themselves in this respect: they know—but cannot provide more specific reasons.

Okay, should I join them in that way of thinking? When wondering whether I know myself to have a free will, say, I might feel as though I'll have to rely on intuiting its presence. Similarly, I could believe that I'm able to solve my intellectual agonizing over how I know this hand to be mine, simply by intuiting its mine-ness. What would this involve? Who can say? Who needs to say? Intuition is inexplicable; or so people tell me.

Over the years, I've met or heard of many people who think of self-knowledge, especially, in this trusting way. "Don't limit your thinking to the rational," I've been advised, "Be more intuitive! Only in that way will you really know yourself." Well, I'm not sure about this. It's suspiciously easy to credit oneself with a capacity for intuitive insight. Doing so would allow one, when facing problems in explaining or understanding an opinion, always to claim to know "through intuition" whether it's true. If this isn't dogmatic, I don't know what is! Someone's believing they have a capacity for intuitive insight doesn't guarantee their belief's being right. How could I know myself to have an intuitive capacity? Would I have to intuit my power of intuition? Will I say, "By intuition," if asked how I know that I know things by intuition? Hopefully, no: that wouldn't be informative. (Of course, *ideas*—possible truths—could occur inexplicably to me. This by itself won't make them knowledge, though. They'll need to be tested or verified by other means—looking, listening, and so on.)

In any event, I'm not sure I do have any inexplicable power of intuition. Can there be good evidence of intuition's presence? Some say so—based on what, though? What would be my evidence for thinking that a belief of mine is supported, even partly, in an inexplicable way? Maybe I would feel myself to be manifesting an instinctive sense of truth. Yet surely that feeling could easily be mistaken. What usually happens, as far as I can tell, is that people accord themselves intuition to explain (even while acknowledging, by talking of intuition in the first place, that they cannot explain!) their surprisingly knowing something. Talk of "intuition" *becomes* an attempted explanation (a self-defeating one, though). If it turns out that their belief about that something was correct, they think like this: "I must have had knowledge, because I had an accurate belief. Yet *how* did I know? Who knows? Still, I must have done so, somehow. Let's call it intuition!" No, let's not: being right about something doesn't prove that one has knowledge, let alone inexplicable knowledge. Maybe that person formed his or her accurate opinion haphazardly, without noticing this flukiness.

Alternatively, the person might unwittingly be using a perfectly proper method—nothing deeply mysterious, just one that he or she doesn't understand. A particular person's not understanding how an opinion is knowledge doesn't show that *no one* could understand it. Modern science provides many models of how progress is possible in understanding what initially seems inexplicable. These days, it seems, there's much scientific understanding of how the world works that wasn't available centuries ago, even to educated people. Even so, I mustn't accord the present period undue importance: are our theories the last word on the world? That's unlikely; scientists are aware of there being much that science doesn't yet comprehend. In many cases, we don't know even how much is know*able*. What people now call "intuition," designating a supposedly unknowable way of know-ing, might be understood quite well in 100 years' time, particularly if science retains its present power and significance for us.

Here's a simple instance of how that kind of transition in understand-ing could begin. Suppose I spend years looking at people's faces, making substantial pronouncements as to their character. I might be extremely reliable at this, generally accurate; and I attribute my success to a deep and inexplicable intuitive power of psychological insight. Others en-courage this belief of mine, praising my "special gift." My reputation grows: police consult me, treating me as a lie detector; the opinions I provide become admissible in courts (and, naturally, a TV show is based on my "amazing life story"). Nonetheless, suppose that the truth is more mundane: I'm very observant at "reading faces," noticing and inter-preting facial mannerisms. (I'm naturally speedy at registering minute facial alterations or "tics"; and I've paid careful attention to faces over many years, unconsciously noting patterns.) It's a useful skill which not everyone possesses; still, it isn't profound and ultimately inexplicable. Probably, once science has noticed enough details, it can even be taught. Imagine that I and others don't yet realize this, however. Sincerely yet mistakenly, we might well continue crediting me with a deeply inexpli-cable ability, "beyond reason."

> *Explicability question.* Why do so many people readily accord them-selves powers of intuition? Should they allow those with whom they disagree to have similar powers?

4.3 Dreams

I won't claim to have self-knowledge through intuition, then. I will try to discover *explicable* methods for gaining self-knowledge. But might people who claim to be helped by intuition be right in the following respect? Maybe self-knowledge can come from *special* or *distinctive* methods for forming or defending accurate opinions. For a while longer, I'll test that idea, because many people believe it's true.

One possibility that's been suggested to me is the phenomenon of dreaming. Often, people are convinced that they can learn significant details about themselves through their dreams (or similarly "unplanned" ways). The widely popularised work of Sigmund Freud (the Austrian originator of psychoanalysis), especially, has convinced generations of earnest inquirers that some of their most personal inner wishes or motivations, say, can be uncovered—hence known—by attending to their dreams. Am I troubled about something, wishing it to end? Of course—if my dreams tell me so. Am I unwittingly sexually insecure? Again, yes—if that's how my dreams should be interpreted. And so on: self-knowledge would be delivered to me while I sleep! (I've heard of late-night TV advertisements promising weight loss while one sleeps. Surprisingly, one needs only to wear the advertiser's product.) Are dreams like windows (well-cleaned ones) looking onto our inner beings?

I don't think so. I doubt that my dreams are a repository of much, if any, knowledge about myself.

First, there is little to prevent me from interpreting my dreams so that they are merely "telling" me whatever it suits me to hear. "Interpretation" is a key term here (as Freud knew). Dreams rarely convey much that's literally true or accurate. They generally portray stuff that's physically impossible! Nor do they include authoritative subtitles or an all-knowing commentary—their "official" interpretation. *Much* interpretation is needed if a dream is to give real knowledge, so that one sees through the symbols, understanding the signs. Yet this sort of interpreting is highly unreliable. It is somewhat speculative, clearly prone to error. Disputes reign among psychoanalysts as to how to interpret dreams. It is a highly theoretical business, and theories have a habit of being incorrect. Over the years, this has been an especially contested area of thought. Are my dreams unambiguously informative? Hardly; most of them are rubbish, as far as I can tell.

To be fair, not all are. Sometimes, I'll think a dream was accurate. Can *these* dreams give me knowledge of myself? Not obviously. When I recognise that what's portrayed in a specific dream is accurate (such as by really reflecting how I'm feeling), I do so by *already* having the knowledge in question about myself. (Suppose I know already that I'm sad. This is why I would then accept, as an accurate representation of me, the sadness I experience in some dream.) In this case, however, I'm not interpreting the dream in a genuinely exploratory way. I wouldn't be relying on it for the knowledge in question. The dream wouldn't be *giving* me the knowledge, in the sense of introducing me to knowledge I didn't already have. It would be "acting out" or vividly "expressing" knowledge I already possess.

Should I therefore ignore my dreams, when seeking self-knowledge? Are they useless in that respect? I can think of two ways in which they might help me to know myself.

A dream might *remind* me of something about myself, such as past events or feelings. ("I'd forgotten how scared I am of heights. I don't want that dream again.") So, a dream could *reawaken* self-knowledge. (I would already, via some other experiences, have known that I'm afraid of heights.) In this way, a dream can prompt my memory—without itself, strictly speaking, being a *source* of the knowledge about myself. (It's not itself a source of the knowledge because, without memory being involved, there wouldn't be knowledge, via the dream, of past events or feelings.)

A dream may also help by giving me a new thought about myself, so that I conceive of myself in a fresh way—with this new thought possibly becoming knowledge at a later time, via a different method. It wouldn't be knowledge while appearing in the dream; nor would it be knowledge simply because it was in a dream. Still, maybe the new thought wouldn't have occurred to me without the dream's intervention; and once it's in my mind, I might be able to transform it into knowledge. How would this happen? Most likely, I would test or support the new thought with further thinking. By undergoing this process, it might become knowledge (if it survives the process). Thus, the dream would provide me with an *idea*, which I might then independently turn into knowledge. This makes dreams potentially useful in self-knowledge, without being a source themselves, strictly speaking, of knowledge. (They could be a source only if an idea can be knowledge *because* it comes from a dream; I don't think this would be so.)

> *Dreaming question.* If no one was ever to have dreams, how would this affect people's senses of reality?

4.4 Literature and movies

Much the same is true, I suspect, of novels, short stories, poems, and movies. Are these ever sources of self-knowledge, providing not only distraction or pleasure, but also genuine personal insight?

Suppose I compare myself to some fictional character. Maybe I recognise myself in him or her: "Yes, that's me. Now I understand that aspect of myself." Then again, I could distance myself from the character: "Thankfully, I'm unlike that person." The novel or, equally, a poem could also eloquently portray a mood or emotion, helping me to clarify what I'm feeling: "Okay. *That* is how I felt. Now I know the feeling more fully, even why I had it." Such reactions can help. They might offer ideas as to how to appreciate or cope with an aspect of life, such as a conflict at work, a romantic involvement, or the like. I have a character, just as a fictional person can *be* a character; and mine could become clearer to me when I'm watching, or reading of, an imagined character's experiences.

Still, it's one thing to clarify options or to welcome new ideas; it's another thing to have knowledge. Would I know myself, in ways I didn't previously, by reacting to a novel or movie with feelings of personal insight? When I was young, I was more likely to think so. My present doubts are philosophical: I don't believe that self-knowledge is simply a matter of having some fresh *conception* of myself, or of how to approach something in my life. No, if I'm going to know myself, this will be by subsequently observing, and thinking about, how that fresh conception works in practice. In other words, *observations* and accompanying *reflections* would give me knowledge. Observation and reflection would be the sources of the self-knowledge. The fiction would, at best, supply ideas. These wouldn't *thereby* be knowledge. (I'm reminded of an academic piety of our time, which is that college or university is primarily about questioning received wisdom and thinking critically—even as the college or university mission statements and mottos talk of the pre-eminent need to gain knowledge. I'm as enthusiastic as anyone about being questioning and critical; but these shouldn't be confused with knowing. They can spark knowing; they can also squelch it.)

A simple instance of that distinction (between a self-conception and some self-knowledge) occurs to me. Very early in my life (I'm told), my mother worried that I might be overly timid, such as when confronted by overgrown areas of our imperfectly controlled garden. For a while, therefore, she read to me, before I went to sleep at night, from the famous fairy tales collected and retold by the Grimm brothers. Importantly, she didn't read me the abridged and sanitized ("child-friendly") versions. No, I fell asleep to the original, unabridged, Grimm fairy tales, including their thrilling but extremely scary details! Grim indeed were the details; almost overwhelming were the challenges faced by their heroes and heroines. Was I scared? I don't recall; presumably so. Was the experience emotionally scarring? On the contrary: there was success! If the young prince could rescue the princess from that forbidding tower, or overcome those dragons, monstrous thorns, and sheer ice, then so could I. Not literally, of course; but the lesson was evident, even to my all-but-unformed mind. Lo and behold: the timidity was gone. Now I charged into parts of the garden I had previously shunned. Result: increased happiness (plus more cuts, bruises, filthiness, and similar adornments of childhood).

What knowledge was I gaining from the stories? Having heard

them, did I then know myself to be braver? I don't think so. Maybe the stories gave me *thoughts* of myself as braver. Only afterwards, however, did I come to know that I was braver; and I did this by observing myself in action—experiencing my running, burrowing, rolling over, and so forth, in places from which I had previously retreated. Simply hearing the stories couldn't have given me this knowledge.

Even so, the stories were important because (I'm accepting, all these years later) they made various kinds of action more likely for me—actions requiring some bravery. The stories probably altered my conception of myself, enlarging the range of possible acts I envisaged as realistic when confronting our garden and elsewhere.

Did the stories therefore give me no new knowledge? Well, if I hadn't heard them, I mightn't have begun thinking in those more confident ways; and maybe I did then know that I had these new thoughts. So, the stories gave me the thoughts; and by knowing of my having these, the stories gave me what I knew *of*. In that sense, they gave me new knowledge. Nevertheless, I didn't *know* of the thoughts because of the stories; I only *had* the thoughts because of the stories. When gaining that new knowledge of having that self-conception, I had this knowledge in a normal way—via introspection, reflecting upon my mind's contents. Yes, the stories put the thoughts there; but the thoughts themselves weren't knowledge because they were caused by stories; and the knowledge of their presence was due to normal introspection. Admittedly, the stories changed me by changing how I was thinking of myself. Yet these changes, these new thoughts, were ones I could know of in a normal way, through introspection.

Literary question. When contemplating our lives, do we conceive of ourselves as being characters in stories (central characters, if we're confident)? Do we think about our lives as aspiring novelists regard their plots and characters? When, if ever, do we begin *reading*, rather than writing, our lives?

4.5   Actions

Much normal self-knowledge which I might gain through observation and reflection would be knowledge of my actions. How simple, though, is it for me to know myself by knowing my actions? How easily may I know an action *as* mine?

That's a fundamental question: what I *do* is vital to what I *am*. That's true of me today, no less so when I was a child. "Know me by my actions," is sound advice. ("Watch what I do, not what I say," is meant to convey the same idea—although it fails, because saying *is* doing. Indeed, saying can be an important kind of action, with character being revealed in what one says.) When contemplating the inevitable ending of my life, I fear it as the ending of my capacity to *do* things. Life should be agency, the ability to do things. I don't live passively, simply being acted upon by aspects of the world (for example, people, other beings, forces). I'm not a mere subject. I'm also an agent, acting in the world—acting "back at" the world in response to its acting upon me. Otherwise, ... well, I cannot imagine that still being me. This doesn't mean my always acting in grand ways, making big movements; little ones suffice. Right now, this body is moving, albeit in tiny ways. This hand isn't moving at the moment, but it feels as if it could. This seems integral to my sense of myself. (Luckily so; paralysis could alter this sense.) If I try imagining this body's never moving, lacking all capacity for self-movement (without having undergone trauma), would I still believe it to be mine? Surely not.

Still, even once it is moving, how do I know it's *my* body moving? This is the question of whether I can have self-knowledge by observing and reflecting upon my actions, recognizing them as mine and no one else's. I continually claim such knowledge—talking of *my* actions, of what *I'm* doing. (The past few days have been full of such thoughts.) Is the situation so straightforward, though?

In answering that question, I'll consider two sorts of case. First, there are actions *already* done or *being* done: in assessing whether the Grimm brothers' stories made me braver, I need to know that I did proceed to crawl among those dark, thick, bushes of my childhood garden. How do I know it was *my* action of burrowing into the undergrowth? Second, there are actions *yet* to be done: how do I know what I will do tomorrow?

Okay, first I'll think about actions I've done or that I'm doing now—specifically, about how I would know these to be mine. The primary case to think about is that of current actions (being done *now*). As to past actions, I would know of them now (as *having* been done by me), by remembering them as having been mine at the time, when they were current actions. So, if I can know an action as being mine when it's current, the normal method of memory might later allow me to know of it as *having* been done by me.

To the primary case, then: how do I know that my hand is moving now, as a present action of mine? I have to do this observationally. The hand I see before me is moving. I say it's "mine," calling the movement "an action of mine." I do this on the basis of appearances. The hand stretches; I feel something. It moves; I feel something. Of course, other hands move; and I sense them, but not as I do my own. What's the difference?

Is it that I see the others only from afar? No: another's hand could be closer than mine to my eyes. (A friend could place his or her hand near my eyes, while I move mine further away.) Would the difference, rather, be my use of the *kinaesthetic* sense? That's the sensing of one's position and movement. The idea is that whenever I'm walking, for instance, I sense my shifting location. Would this mean having a sense of my own walking that I lack of anyone else's? Well, I'm imagining ... right now ... closing my eyes and covering my ears while walking. I'll neither see nor hear anyone else walking. Would a sense of my own walking remain, with a clearly defined sense of my positions as I move? Scientific studies don't make this clear. They suggest that kinaesthetic verdicts rely heavily on introspection, memory, and visual data (such as accumulated associations between visual information about spatial distributions and internal feelings of the movements of joints). Possibly, then, kinaesthesia isn't really independent of vision. In any case, it's not clear how *reliable* kinaesthetic data are: they are complex, for a start.

So, I don't know what to make of this kind of case. If there isn't a special way of knowing, purely from within, my own actions *as* my own, maybe I'll have to revisit my concerns from Day 1. Back then, it seemed that my efforts to sense my body as being mine—observing it "from outside," using the usual senses—raised doubts and questions as to whether I *could* know this body as mine. Is it easier to know my body by knowing it in action, and "from within"? That's what I've been asking just now; clearly, questions remain.

Conceivably, I'll have more success by thinking about actions I'm yet to do. Let's see. Often I do seem to know of these in advance of their occurring. How could this happen? Here, *intention* might seem to be the key. If I intend acting in a particular way, I can be confident that I'll therefore act in that way. Is this confidence thereby knowledge, in advance, of what I'll do?

For instance, do I know I'm going to raise my hand in two minutes time? (Looking intently at my watch, right now, I intend doing so.) Like everyone else, I attribute such knowledge to myself in ordinary settings. Are those attributions ever accurate? Yesterday's analysis of knowledge could allow them to be. Here's how that analysis would supply that verdict. First, I can be confident I'll raise my hand. Second, this confidence could be accurate, even now, because in fact I will proceed to raise my hand. Third, my confidence could be reliable, and backed by good evidence, with nothing in the circumstances being likely to prevent my raising my arm.

Is that all there is to it? Possibly so, although I must remember that this self-knowledge would be knowledge of the future. Many people tell me that no one *can* ever know the future. They would deny, for example, that I know that my country's political leader isn't about to begin crazily dancing during a grand official ceremony. I don't believe this will happen; yet it could. How do I know it won't? (That feels like a substantial question. So, something still needs to be solved here. Perhaps I'll think more about this odd sort of possibility tomorrow.)

> *Action question.* Approximately how many actions would an "average" hour of manual activity include? Approximately how many actions would an "average" hour of sleep include?

4.6 Psychological and medical studies

Today, I've contemplated how I might know myself "from within"—examining my subjective sense of myself. Might some self-knowledge come "from outside," though? Maybe I should try viewing myself as others do. I suspect that an "external" perspective on me might sometimes be a *more* reliable source of accurate beliefs about me (more reliable than my "internal" perspective on myself).

After all, I cannot always rely on introspecting, or even observing, myself. For instance, when asking myself whether I possess some personal characteristic, such as patience, I might receive a confused reply, due to not having a clear and consistent bunch of observations of myself: I haven't always paid sufficiently careful attention to myself. Even when trying to rectify that, I could end up with a jumble of competing thoughts and impressions. On one day, I'll act patiently; another day, I won't. How may these conflicting data be reconciled? I mightn't always know.

It's also possible to misread data within one's mind, such as by misinterpreting one feeling for another. It's notoriously difficult to know whether one is feeling love, for example, or merely infatuation (perhaps only a physical attraction). More depressingly, think of a person who claims to love another even when abusing him or her. I doubt the abuser understands what love is, no matter how earnestly he or she claims to do so. Love is never a punch or a kick to the guts, let alone repeated ones. The abusive person's not understanding this shows how useless introspection is, in this instance, for revealing whether he or she loves the unfortunate partner. It's from outside the abuser's mind (much the best place to be!) that his or her lack of love is known.

Take another example—anger. When consulting inner feelings, one might "just know" that one is angry at another person—except that this inner confidence needn't be knowledge at all. Seemingly, one can be angry at oneself without realizing it, turning the anger upon the most convenient alternative target. I've sometimes done this; independent experts would recognise the pattern. (It is probably they who would even conceive of the possibility of the anger's not really being as it feels to the person experiencing it.)

Examples like these prompt the question of whether self-knowledge is possible in such situations only by adopting or consulting "external" perspectives. Thus, by reading a psychology textbook or a medical reference book, I might learn much about myself. I would "step outside" myself, ceasing to think of myself only "from within." Just another person—that's me! This is what I would find. Do I live in a way that I understand just by knowing how I *feel*, for instance? Definitely not: I cannot know everything about myself by "looking within." This should be no surprise, really, since I'm part of a "public" world. There are respects in which I would be better viewed "from outside." I'll know about myself in these respects only if others can do so.

Is this spooky? Not at all. Nor is it like being under constant hidden camera surveillance, because no one need be studying me in particular unless I request it; and when researchers study others, this can still help me to know myself. By listening to radio, watching TV, or reading appropriate books, I can learn of the research results (in simplified versions). In effect, I can treat myself *as if* I've been studied. ("They studied people in the following sort of situation: ... That's my situation. I'll read on.")

Accordingly, an "external" perspective can help me to learn about myself. I follow this approach routinely when listening respectfully to a doctor. In a way, I *want* the doctor to treat me as not unique. I hope I'm recognizable to him or her as someone whose body acts like other bodies, ones already studied. Yes, the doctor should notice my details, to align these with studies by medical researchers of other people who've had these symptoms. This is what good doctors do; and I accept its often being the best way to know my body—"from outside." I'll then know about these aspects of myself, only if these other people could already do so. I'll learn from what others say. (Of course, the doctor might be baffled. Then he or she might refer me to a specialist. Could a neuroscientist, for example, gain knowledge of my moods and motivations that I lack? Probes of my brain might be the best means of knowing such aspects of me!)

Worried question. Is a person who barely passes his or her medical exams a medical authority or expert? (Remember that half of all doctors finished in the bottom half of their graduating medical class.)

4.7 *Friends and family*

Not only "official" experts are potentially helpful in that way. I don't ask my doctor about everything regarding myself. Psychology is still developing as a discipline; I don't always consult psychology books anyway. (And "self-help" books are rarely very intelligent.) Where else might I turn for knowledge about myself?

At times, I seek advice from people who know me more "intimately"—usually, friends and my wife. I'm hoping they know me in some way I don't know myself. Their views aren't inherently special or always correct; but their "external" perspective on me is something I don't clearly possess. This could be significant if I'm "losing" perspective on myself. Do I often lack the required "detachment" from myself? That's all too possible, for me as for anyone.

Of course, there's no guarantee of success in talking to these well-meaning people. Friends and family aren't wholly detached. I would ask for their advice because they care about me (and are therefore more likely to have noticed much about me). However, this strength has a weakness. People who care about me will want not to think ill of me by being critical; and this desire could affect the likely accuracy of their more substantial claims about me. It's reassuring to think that because they care about me, they'll be reliable in their views of me. Yet (for the same reason) this optimistic thought of mine needn't be true.

There's another reason for caution, too, in how much credibility I accord such people's views of me. Although they have spent time around me, is that sufficient for understanding me? Probably not. In understanding me, they need to understand much more besides. An unintelligent or unworldly friend, no matter how well-meaning, remains unintelligent or unworldly. All of us have limitations in our understanding of the world; and to understand a particular person requires understanding of the larger world. If a friend's knowledge of human nature in general is quite flawed, his or her knowledge of my nature in particular is probably no better! He or she would observe aspects of me without knowing how to interpret them accurately.

Here's another problem, about consulting more than one person: different people tend to offer mutually conflicting views. Whom should I believe? No one is all-knowing. Each of us is fallible: everyone makes mistakes. So, people I consult won't always agree with each other. Some might be right on one issue, while others are best believed on others; and I won't always know who's right on a given occasion. Is there is a *single* authority on all issues (one "guru friend")? None that I know! How can I reliably reconcile different perspectives I might encounter? I could well fail to do so, losing my way in much well-meant but warring advice. Self-knowledge is unlikely to emerge from this morass.

There's a deeper problem, too. Whatever I'm told by others, I must reflect upon, if it's to give me self-knowledge. Yet how do I know what's accurate in what I'm hearing, without *already* knowing myself in these respects? In practice, this can mean my believing only those who tell me what I already believe about myself. It is they who will seem to me to be correct, after all! However, this is hardly a reliable way of learning new truths about myself. It risks merely entrenching my existing opinions about myself. These needn't be knowledge.

> Friendship question. Is it possible for someone to be my friend while knowing little about me? Could someone know too *much* about me to be my friend?

4.8 Experience and maturity

Maybe self-knowledge arises more easily with maturity. As wrinkles arrive, when hairs become grey and eyes weaken, is there compensation in knowing more about oneself? In theory, one knows more of the world by spending more time in it. Possibly, one knows more of oneself (part of the world, after all) by spending more time *being* oneself. Do trials and errors inseparable from growing older increase one's self-knowledge (such as of one's character)?

Not necessarily: experience doesn't always teach us what should be learned from it. I could make the same sort of mistake repeatedly, never noticing (let alone correcting) the avoidable pattern. Simply by biologically persisting, by living, I'll undergo experiences and I'll mature—at least in a shallow sense. Yet what do I learn from these experiences? This question touches upon the *quality* of how I mature. There seem to be respects in which I have more accurate beliefs about myself, and the world in general, than I did when young. Certainly, I reason better now than then. I also observe much that, previously, I wasn't capable of noticing. (Many details begin falling into patterns that catch one's attention only with careful experience.) Much of my observing is more discerning than it used to be.

Nevertheless, not all is progress. I'm unsure whether my memory is better now than when I was young. (I can't now remember exactly how good it was then!) Definitely, some of my senses aren't as powerful and accurate as in the past. Maybe, too, there are respects in which *no one* can improve. In today's musing, I've been loath to credit myself with having as many independent ways of gaining self-knowledge as some people think they possess. Along the way, I've mentioned possible limitations upon how I would gain self-knowledge. What strikes me is the seeming impossibility of eliminating all those potential problems.

Thus, today's thinking began by accepting that I'll never know for sure how I've come to have a particular opinion—no matter *what* age I am. (The same worry applies to *defending* a particular opinion.) The problem was one of principle, not mere practicality—afflicting any-one at any time of life. I also decided that dreams, novels, and the like are not—and (I'll now add) never could be—special sources of self-knowledge. This is so, irrespective of age or maturity. Nor will I ever, even when older, have a different way of knowing myself through my actions: I'll still need to sense my body or introspect my intentions; this basic need won't change, I believe, as I grow older. Questions and doubts will therefore remain, even about knowing what I am by know-ing what I do. How can I know *what* I've done, am doing, or am going to do? Becoming older also won't remove limitations upon how much I can know myself by "looking within." External perspectives on myself will continue being needed—even while continuing not to provide all the answers.

Moreover, at no age will a whole new way of knowing myself sud-denly be granted to me; that's how it appears right now, at any rate. I find it hard to believe (without indulging in wishful thinking) that a special way of knowing will arrive, simply by my growing older. The most I hope for is that I may further refine my powers of observing and of reasoning (even as aspects of these will probably worsen with age), applying these to social situations, to beliefs about people and the world in general. Maybe I'll understand better my own roles within such situations, and my own significance among people and the world as a whole. Even so, I'll still use those same underlying general methods: I'll observe, remember, and reason. I'll exercise these more or less well; and none of them will remove all the barriers to self-knowledge I've described over these four days.

Those are somewhat sombre thoughts. Should they be deeply disturbing? Do they describe a plight, or just a feature? They point to limitations; and so I have to wonder whether those limitations seriously undermine how we think of ourselves and our capacity for self-knowledge.

Tomorrow, I'll ponder that sort of question more fully. For the moment, though: one implication worth noting is that older people needn't even know *more* about the world, or about people as a whole, than some younger people do. Limitations cloak everyone, regardless of age. No one is always right, particularly on significant matters. No one possesses perfect insight into the world or themselves. Growing older doesn't alter that. Growing older needn't constitute, or result in, progress as a knower; and, again, it isn't a special method of knowing.

Developmental question. Does intelligence get "lost" if not used well? (Does it wither without such use?) Is it also strengthened by good use?

4.9 Back to basics

Today, I've thought about possible *sources* of self-knowledge, potential ways of satisfying yesterday's analysis of self-knowledge. Where do I find myself now, at day's end?

I've confronted a few recurrent themes. It seems that I know myself, if I do, through observation (this might include kinaesthesia), memory, and reflection (this could encompass introspection). For example, I need to observe, remember, and reflect upon how I act within the world—what I've done and what I intend doing. Observing what others say or write, too, will help—hearing or reading, and reflecting upon, whatever they can impart about how we fit into the world. (This can include attending to their *testimony*, certainly a source of many of my beliefs, even about myself.) To an extent, therefore, *self*-knowledge would be knowledge of the *surrounding* world. It isn't knowledge only of myself. This result fits well with yesterday's guiding thoughts. I've seen, in more detail, ways in which self-knowledge is like knowledge of other aspects of the world (along with differences, of course).

I've noticed ways of getting *ideas* about myself—dreams, novels, films, poems, testimony, and so on—which, nonetheless, aren't obviously sources of self-knowledge themselves. Converting some of these ideas into real knowledge will require combinations of observation, memory, and reflection. Accuracy and normal reliability will need to be involved; and so people's *beliefs* about themselves probably won't always be knowledge about themselves. Not only that; if *only* the standard sources—observation, memory, and reflection—happen to have the normal reliability needed for self-knowledge, then people's knowledge of themselves probably won't always be what they *wish* to know about themselves. It could be quite mundane (such as knowledge of this hand's being mine). It needn't be profound or exciting (such as knowledge provided only by a deeply revelatory dream).

Hierarchy question. Is one of our various senses more important than the others for knowing the world?

4.10 Tomorrow, into battle

Wait a moment: those final remarks might be dangerously blasé about ordinary self-knowledge! Many people who have almost died will, afterwards, regard nothing within ordinary life as mundane: "Yes, I know it's my hand. Isn't this marvellous? I'm happy to be alive with that hand." Why do I mention that case? It's because tomorrow, finally, I'm going to confront a dramatic possibility—the possible failure, the "death," of my attempts to gain self-knowledge.

I'm already anticipating that battle of ideas, and I'm excited. (Admittedly, it's dangerous, because I don't know how it will end; but that uncertainty—along with the "high stakes" involved—is invigorating.) I'll be asking, genuinely, whether I *lack* all self-knowledge. Today I've remained optimistic about that, analysing examples accordingly. Yet have I been too optimistic, too unreflective, too uncritical?

That's what I plan to ask in detail tomorrow. I'm hoping that it will be my final test within these meditations—pushing me to decide whether, even after my efforts during the past four days, I *can* have self-knowledge.

> *Introspective question.* I can't see myself seeing, unless a mirror allows this. (But can I ever touch myself touching myself, or smell myself smelling myself, and so on? Seemingly not.) Even unaided, though, I can think I'm thinking. Does this difference between sensing and thinking show that introspection plays a special role in giving me self-knowledge?

4.11   Overview of the day

Today's reasoning has tested these hypotheses:

> There are no methods for gaining self-knowledge.

> Alternatively, there are methods for gaining self-knowledge, including: inexplicable intuition; dreams, fiction, movies, and the like; attending to one's actions; listening to others' views (either explicitly or implicitly) on oneself; experience and maturity.

What emerged from those tests? This hypothesis did:

> If there is self-knowledge, it is gained, strictly speaking, via observation (perhaps including testimony), memory, and reflection.

Questions remain, of course, including these:

> If I lacked all capacity for memory, could I only know myself at a particular time? Would that not *be* real knowledge? Must knowledge be able to be retained for a while? (If an opinion fades as soon as it appears, is it not really knowledge, even briefly?) Consider the contrasting possibility (which is a few people's actual plight) of forgetting nothing one has done or experienced. In that case, would one never know oneself (due to being incapable of organising the mass of memory data)? Must self-knowledge therefore be selective in what it observes and remembers? However, if there is conscious selecting, could a *self-serving* picture develop? Alternatively, if there is unconscious selecting, could a *random* picture appear? In either case, is self-knowledge unlikely to be the result?

FURTHER READING

Today's initial focus, in §4.1, was upon the *generality* problem (as it is typically termed): how is only *one* method being used in forming or maintaining a particular opinion or belief? On this, see Conee and Feldman, "The Generality Problem for Reliabilism," in *Evidentialism* (Oxford: Oxford University Press, 2004).

Then intuition, as a method of gaining knowledge, was examined in §4.2. For remarks on it, see Quine and Ullian, *The Web of Belief* (New York: Random House, 1970), pp. 60-61; and Alvin Goldman, *Epistemology and Cognition* (Cambridge, MA: Harvard University Press, 1986), pp. 285-86.

The next few sections (§§4.3-4.8) tested other possible suggestions for "everyday" methods of gaining self-knowledge. On Freud on self-knowledge via dreams (§4.3), see Richard Wollheim's *Freud* (London: Fontana, 1973), pp. 66-79. On literature and knowing oneself (§4.4), see Martha Nussbaum, "Fictions of the Soul," in her *Love's Knowledge* (New York: Oxford University Press, 1990). On knowledge, in advance, of one's actions (§4.5), see Stuart Hampshire's *Freedom of the Individual*, 2nd edition (London: Chatto and Windus, 1975), chapter 3; and Anne Newstead's "Knowledge by Intention: On the Possibility of Agent's Knowledge", in Stephen Hetherington (ed.), *Aspects of Knowing* (Oxford: Elsevier, 2006). On whether testimony (§4.6) is a basic source of knowledge, see C.A.J. Coady's *Testimony* (Oxford: Oxford University Press, 1992).

The day's thinking ended (§4.9) by indicating briefly what philosophers would typically believe to be knowledge-gathering methods *underlying* the above ways of forming opinions. For more on the methods (such as reasoning, introspection, memory, and perception) that philosophers usually believe to be our *basic* ones for gaining knowledge, see, for example, Robert Audi's *Epistemology*, 2nd edition (New York: Routledge, 2003), Part I. For classic arguments as to the importance of such sources, see Plato's *Meno*, 79e-86c (on reason and memory); Descartes's "Meditation II" (on introspection and reason); Locke's *Essay Concerning Human Understanding*, Book I, chapter 2, Sections 1-5, 12-16, and Book II, chapter 1, Sections 1-5 (on perception and introspection); and Hume's *Enquiry Concerning Human Understanding* (1748), §§I, II (on perception, memory, and introspection).

DAY 5 | CONFRONTING DOUBTS ABOUT WHETHER SELF-KNOWLEDGE IS POSSIBLE

We shall not cease from exploration
And the end of all our exploring
Will be to arrive where we started
And to know the place for the first time.

T.S. Eliot, "Little Gidding," in *Four Quartets*

5.1 Doubts, more doubts

Today's the day: to know myself, or not to know myself? For four days, I've been thinking hard about this, often feeling pessimistic as to my prospects. It's been puzzling, intense, and worrying. Days 1 and 2 were full of doubts—which I cannot, in all honesty, pretend I've completely solved. Now, more await. I'll begin today, at any rate, by subjecting myself to further doubts. (I've woken, eager to confront these.)

Why would I do that, though? (It's hardly going to make today relaxing!) I'll do it because I should: it's intellectually important. I'll be approaching these doubts in an experimental and inquiring spirit, respecting two significant possibilities, each of which bears upon the intellectual integrity of these meditations.

First, there is the possibility that I'll end by deciding that I *cannot* have self-knowledge. That would be a pity, an unwelcome outcome. So, it had better be a conclusion I *have* to accept, if I'm to accept it at all. It had better reflect a sustained pattern of unanswerable doubts—not casual thinking or easily avoidable doubts.

Equally, I hope not to reach too glibly for the conclusion I do want—which is that I *can* have some self-knowledge. I should walk away with that comforting conviction only if I've really *tested* it, by evaluating seriously and open-mindedly the thought that self-knowledge *isn't* possible. Otherwise, the question would linger of whether I had overcome the *strongest* doubts—so that I would really *deserve* the result I want. If I haven't overcome the strongest doubts I can imagine or of which I've heard, then I shouldn't, in good intellectual faith, be wholly confident of having self-knowledge. Perhaps I would be believing only what's convenient or comforting; and *that* isn't a reliable route to truth. So, I must open my mind, for a while longer, to some probing doubts.

> *Doubt question.* Are some doubts more substantial than others? Is there a guaranteed way to know when a doubt merits respect?

5.2   Sensing and observing

Day 1 raised doubts about what self-knowledge I could obtain by observing myself. I asked how, by using my senses, I could know this body as mine; and I had problems, notably when seeking to observe this body's mine-ness.

Well, how reliable are *anyone's* senses, as a source of *any* accurate beliefs? Senses are never wholly reliable. Short-sightedness isn't rare. Nor is long-sightedness. People can have poor hearing, not to mention less-than-perfectly discerning senses of smell, taste, and so on. In any event, no one has perfect hearing, sight, and the rest. Let's not forget sensory illusions and hallucinations, either; everyone is vulnerable to these. Roads seem to ripple under the sun's heat; sticks appear to bend when entering a glass of water. In such cases, what we seem to sense is something we *only* seem to sense. We can be misled.

Observation in a broader sense is also imperfect. People talk of someone's "powers of observation," meaning more than the ability to sense accurately—meaning the ability to notice accurately and discerningly (for example, seeing the vital detail) from among whatever material arises through one's senses. Am I good at observing what's important in my surroundings? Not always. Even what's "in front of my face" can escape my notice. While travelling, for example, it's easy to sense, without observing, the passing vista. Minds "switch off," no longer registering much.

> Sensing question. Is there a limit to how much sensory information one can absorb, with which to gain knowledge of one's surroundings?

5.3 Reasoning and memory

Will "pure" powers of reasoning fare better? Are they immune to doubts? No such luck. One possible weakness in reason's armour is its reliance, in practice, upon memory.

Here's a simple example. I'll imagine someone spending hours trying to solve a substantial problem in logic; and I'll suppose that this person is the best logician ever, relying only upon "pure reason" (that is, nothing sensory). Even this person might make mistakes. He or she needs to consider and compare alternative possibilities, holding much in mind—with ideas coming in and out of thought. This takes time. Even brilliant reasoning involves memory, with earlier steps being stored, awaiting evaluation and use. And memory isn't wholly reliable, unable to mislead (especially when complex thinking is involved). As the thinking progresses, one needs to remember earlier stages of it.

This is relevant to self-knowledge. Most of my reasoning on Days 1 and 2 was complicated; and I need to recall it if I'm to evaluate its implications. Subtle reasoning is needed, as is memory. (Yesterday, I wondered whether intuition could be used instead, to gain "immediate" insight. This idea wasn't useful.) Wherever subtle reasoning is present, there is marked potential for mistakes, if only because the reasoning takes time.

> *Memory question.* Do some beliefs or opinions not involve memory (even if it is only remembering parts of a language)?

5.4 Complexity

Not all aspects of me, ones I try introspecting or observing, are simple. This matters: there are limits to what my mind can accomplish, even in thinking about myself. (Even introspection, therefore, is subject to these limits.)

For instance, suppose I want to attribute to myself the important character trait of consistency in my thinking and acting. It sounds like a simple trait. How would I know its presence? I must reason, reflecting upon my personal history—my life as a whole, what I've said and thought, my actions in general. In practice, however, I can't remember all this. Once more, my limited memory handicaps me.

There's another barrier, too, to gaining such self-knowledge. Even if I could recall everything I've ever done and thought, it would be ridiculously difficult for me to test *all* these for consistency with each other. I couldn't do it. My mind isn't powerful enough. I would be comparing each belief or action with each other one, seeking inconsistencies. How would I do this? It isn't just a "gut instinct" in each case. Thoughtful and careful comparison between all beliefs and actions is required. Perhaps some awareness of logic could help me to begin the task; how would I finish it? I don't think I can; in which case, not all my thoughts and actions will be checked. I'll never know, then, that I've lived consistently.

Wait a moment; this is only my not knowing that I've lived *completely* consistently. Few people claim such perfection. Can I know I've been *very* (even if not perfectly) consistent, such as in how I've treated other people? Gee. Even this requires a dauntingly large assessment of my thoughts and actions. So, I cannot say conclusively that there's been even a *good* degree of consistency in how I've thought and acted so far. (Moreover, some of my life is still to come, I hope. Suppose that, somehow, I do know myself to have been consistent until now. Would this let me know, by inference, that I'll continue being consistent? This inference would be "inductive"; I intend discussing it soon.)

Spacious question. How large is my mind? What determines this?

5.5 Meaning

Much of my reflection during the past few days has been introspective. I've "looked within," finding opinions and beliefs; then I've tested them, trying to build a knowledgeable conception of myself. Now here's a perplexing question. *Can* I know my mind in this quiet way—my thoughts, commitments, attitudes, goals, and the like? Can I do so, *even* when the thoughts in question seem simple?

Introspecting involves knowing—purely by thinking—what one is thinking. People tend to assume that this is a straightforward way of gaining indubitable self-knowledge (admitting of no coherent and rational doubts). I've often heard reasoning like this:

> They're my own thoughts. So, I cannot fail to know what they mean. They mean whatever I take or intend them to mean. They aren't answerable to anyone else's opinions or interpretations. (No one else could be more right than me about what I mean.)

Is that correct, though? After all, I don't totally control what gives meaning to my thoughts. So I *am* answerable to others, even in understanding my own thinking.

Why so? What I "hear *within*" my mind are words, either in sentences or not—parts of some language, like many I hear *around* me, from others' mouths. Mainly, I'm hearing words of English within me. I'm thereby hearing words from a shared language, a public language. The fact that, at a particular time, they are inside me, not outside, doesn't change this.

This is significant, because English is a language I had to learn, by gaining knowledge of how to use it. (This sort of knowledge is skill in using a language. Some reflective knowledge about the language is also involved.) And this knowledge has limitations: I haven't learned the language perfectly. Although people generally claim to speak a language perfectly, they're being imprecise. I doubt they're literally perfect in their command of the language. At any rate, I make mistakes of grammar and meaning, even in the privacy of my own mind. This isn't surprising: why wouldn't I make such mistakes, given that I make mistakes with the language when speaking or writing it? (At the time, I mightn't notice making them; but that's no proof of not having done so.) Thus, it's possible that I'll unwittingly fail to be thinking what I think I'm thinking! Much could go awry in my thinking, when attempting to frame thoughts and capture meanings. As I said, there's genuine skill to this. Routinely, I assume I'm skilful enough; maybe in fact I'm not. I could be *okay* at using language for my thinking, without being *perfect* or even *excellent* at doing so.

As I try to understand this confronting possibility, the following analogy might help. It's about the widespread confusion between expressing and creating. Almost everyone in the performing arts (let alone the entertainment industry in general), it seems, calls themselves creative. I don't think they are; at best, most are expressive. Being expressive involves being *minimally* creative—giving voice to something that otherwise wouldn't have existed, where this "something" needn't be anything more than a particular person's saying or singing the words in question (instead of someone else's doing so). That's a limited form of creativity! In this sense, *any* sound, gesture, or mark is a creation. *Substantial* creativity goes well beyond this. Performers' feeling that they've created something substantial doesn't prove that they have actually done so.

There is a simple analogy, then, between substantial meaning and substantial creativity. Each has an objective or public aspect. I'm not necessarily meaning anything definite, purely by making sounds in my mind. I need to be using appropriate sounds, for example, in apt ways— so that the sounds have a specific meaning. In order for this to occur, the sounds I use answer to those made by companion speakers of English. It's not up to me, on my own, to create meanings, even within my mind. One sign of this is how easily I could be unsure of the meaning of a word that occurs to me; in which event, I'll check with other people. Normally, I don't need to do this—a fact that can beguile me into thinking that, normally, what's meant by thoughts in my mind *is* wholly up to me. (Even if I choose which words to think, I'm not thereby creating their meanings.) There's an alternative explanation of my rarely consulting others as to what I mean—which is that, even within my own mind, I rarely go beyond "public" words, ones I've heard elsewhere. Occasionally, maybe playfully or professionally, I make up a word or two. Still, I understand or explain even these by linking them with words of English.

Given all that, here's the question I'm facing. If I have failings in my grasp of English (or whatever other public language I use), doesn't this imply failings in my grasp of whatever is in my mind? Might I actually use some words incorrectly, at least somewhat, even in my own mind? The worry is that using words wholly correctly anywhere (in my mind, in speech, or in writing) requires me either to use or adapt a public language; and this needn't be done perfectly. Genuine mistakes—certainly small ones, maybe large ones—are possible, especially without my noticing them.

It's easy to imagine how, in practice, such mistakes would enter the story: potential for error has been present from the outset. I need only reflect upon how I would have learned the public language in the first place. Maybe there is linguistic knowledge with which children are born (as the contemporary linguist Noam Chomsky has argued), such as some grasp of grammar. However, not all linguistic knowledge is innate in that way. Vocabulary isn't. Constituting most of the meaning in sentences, it's learned more slowly, through forms of observation. Like others, I learned English partly by listening and looking—reading, hearing others use or explain words, being corrected in my own word-usage. So, even in knowing what I'm thinking, I draw upon this observational legacy. Am I therefore—indeed, have I always been—vulnerable to mistakes? Surely so. I can misapply words and misshape concepts; I might be insensitive to what these really mean. Earlier today, I described several doubts about observation, about whether it definitely gives me knowledge. Now those same doubts could affect even my knowing what it is that I'm thinking!

Gee. That thought makes me wonder whether *every* aspect of me is answerable to observation. Clearly, my body is part of the observable world. I'm now thinking that my *thoughts*, by having real meanings, might also be part of that world: in order even to understand my own thoughts, it seems, I must call upon my observations of how English is used.

And if that's so, there is a danger to ponder—because the observable world is one about which, in general, I can be mistaken. If my thoughts are part of that world, I could be mistaken even about what thoughts I am ever having!

Meaning question. Could someone invent an entire language, without already understanding another language (a shared or public one)? Are some public languages better, as languages, than others?

5.6 Inductive reasoning

Even if observation is vital to knowing much (including mental aspects of myself), how far can it take me towards knowing the world and myself? Simply observing the here-and-now will never be enough for all the knowledge people seek. We make claims that look further afield; but *can* one have knowledge of more than whatever one has observed?

In practice, people assume so. Observations are often used as data, in inferences moving far beyond those data. One important role for observations is in giving people guidance, hopefully knowledge, as to how best to live. For this, people need a realistic idea of some likely future patterns in their lives. Can such ideas ever be knowledge?

In thinking about this, I'll begin cautiously, looking ahead only to tomorrow. What circumstances will I be in then? How will I act? Answering these questions calls for inductive reasoning—predicting or extrapolating from what I've observed so far. Yet *can* such reasoning give me knowledge, even of tomorrow?

My inductive reasoning extrapolates from evidence of what I've observed, reaching a belief or opinion about something similar that I haven't observed (perhaps because it hasn't yet happened; in which case, I'm making an inductive *prediction*). I believe that I'll eat breakfast tomorrow; but is this belief knowledge? It would be inductive knowledge; and people routinely claim knowledge like this. Similarly, I believe that I'll continue acting well towards my wife; but is this belief knowledge? It would be inductive knowledge; and people standardly say they know such things about themselves. In these cases, I'm reasoning inductively, using my observations as a basis for inferring a continuation of whatever patterns they report. Inductive thinking expects "more of the same," based upon past observations. In everyday life, we rely greatly on such thinking.

Even so, I remember, David Hume famously discovered an inherent weakness within it.

First, he analysed the structure of inductive thinking. If asked how I know I'm going to eat breakfast tomorrow, I'll reply that I have lots of relevant observational evidence. There are memories of past days, each beginning with breakfast. Maybe I recall past intentions to maintain this pattern, intentions upon which I then acted; and I notice having that intention now. Is that my only evidence here? Not quite. Another belief is also being used (even if unconsciously). It's the belief that this is a normal situation, into which nothing will intervene to thwart my intention of having breakfast tomorrow. (Without this extra belief, I wouldn't be confident that I'll have breakfast tomorrow.) Still, how is this extra belief supported? I'm wondering whether it is knowledge (rather than merely a natural belief to have).

Hume would have refused me this knowledge. Certainly, he would have denied that I can know *for sure* that the extra belief is accurate. After all (he would have noted), the world needn't continue being like it has been so far. What I believe to be normal—because until now it has been the world's usual pattern—could be about to change. I might hope this won't occur; but hoping isn't the same as knowing. Nothing I can do now eliminates the possibility of this kind of change occurring in the future, even overnight. I could wake tomorrow to a substantially altered world. Whatever I've observed the world to be like in the past doesn't guarantee its being like that in the future. (As investment advisors routinely proclaim, disingenuously, past success is no guarantee of future success!)

This sort of doubt also applies to self-knowledge. Do I know for sure how my body will react tomorrow? I cannot conclusively rule out its being about to function differently. (Think of many allergies: suddenly, then everlastingly, one's body is vulnerable to them.) What about my knowing for sure how I will *act* tomorrow? No: intentions may change, and they can be frustrated by suddenly altered circumstances. Do I know for sure how I will *think* tomorrow? Again, no: I cannot be sure even of how I'll be thinking in one hour's time!

Would-have question. Can a person know his or her mind only by knowing how it *would have* reacted in various actual or possible circumstances? (How *does* one know this?)

5.7   Test case: love

Here is an experiment. I'll combine some of the doubts I've discussed. Possibly, they interact, producing even "larger" doubts. A test case would be useful. All right, here's one: can a person know that he or she *loves* another?

Yesterday's reflections tell me to answer this, first of all, by thinking of possible *methods* for gaining that sort of knowledge. Most people, I assume, would recommend introspection: "Look within for that certain feeling, the powerful emotion of being in love."

I'm unsure about whether a feeling-at-a-time would be enough evidence. Perhaps love involves some sort of strong tendency, looking towards the future. One would have a commitment, for example, to act in appropriate ways in various situations, including ones yet to arise; and this commitment wouldn't be a mere feeling of commitment. It won't be discovered in its entirety at a single time, by "looking within." I would need to wait, observing my actions in different situations *over* some time: "Did I comfort my wife when she needed it? Was I enjoying her company at the beach?" Asking such questions is far from seeking only a "magical" feeling within oneself at a particular moment.

Nor need it be easy for me to know that I possess this sort of on-going tendency or commitment. People are often confident of knowing they're in love; awkwardly, though, the kinds of doubt I've been noticing apply here.

Thus, suppose I say that love is indeed a feeling—but, I agree, a lasting one. (It's only present *now* if it's also present at *other* times.) Then I might check whether it has been present for a while. I try to remember; and immediately mistakes are possible! For instance, in thinking I've consistently cared deeply for my wife, I might simplify, thereby falsifying, the relevant history of my feelings. Perhaps I'm forgetting times of not caring about her. This "smoothing" of the history might occur because I want to love her—yet don't. For varying reasons, memory can mislead. (I'm not saying it has done so in this case. I'm describing a possibility.)

Can I correct for that possibility, by always knowing for sure whether it's actual in a given situation? Not completely. No matter what evidence I use, and no matter how hard I think, doubts are possible. Here's one: maybe I don't completely understand the general nature of love. If there are gaps or lacks in my knowledge of what love is, maybe I cannot ever be sure I'm in love.

There are further doubts to confront. If knowing myself to be in love must include knowing part of the future (how I *will* feel and act towards the other person), it would be inductive knowledge. Thus, to some extent my knowing I'm in love would be an implicit prediction, concerning how I will continue feeling and acting. I *want* and *intend* to continue acting and feeling lovingly; but there's no guarantee that I will. Do I doubt myself? Well, if the knowledge in question would be inductive, then at least I lack *conclusive* knowledge (what I've been calling "knowledge for sure") of my future feelings and actions.

For example, I would have to know, on the basis of past actions and thoughts, that I'm not about to *stop* loving my wife. Yet nothing that's happened until now can entirely remove this possibility. Presumably, my wife could change dramatically overnight, awaking tomorrow with new attitudes and values, ones abhorrent to me; and I might cease loving her in that circumstance.

Equally, even if my wife doesn't change overnight, *I* might. For no apparent reason, I would no longer be tender and supportive. Do I know that this won't suddenly happen? Not conclusively; it *could* occur. (The fact that I don't want it to happen is beside the point.)

In such ways, therefore, I don't know conclusively that the world isn't about to change from what, so far, it has been observed to be like. In effect, there's a way in which this does happen, as part of initially "growing up," then of maturing further. How one interprets, thereby "seeing," the world can alter greatly, and in unexpected ways, as one changes oneself. In an instant, what has seemed witty or important might now strike one as trite or immature; or now, for the first time, one sees detail and depth in what was previously unappreciated. How one perceives one's partner could be affected by such transformations.

Or is love partly a *decision*—an action? ("I'll open myself emotionally to this person. I will trust her.") Maybe one partly creates love in a deliberate way, as against only discovering it. Even so, there could be doubts. What will show me that it is love I'm creating, or deciding upon—rather than something related (such as admiration or gratitude)? Even when *feeling* as though I'm creating love, surely I could be misreading myself. This would be an action, after all, described to myself in language; and I must admit, I feel, that this attempt could be misunderstood by me (in ways I tried describing earlier).

> *Improvement question.* Would it be possible, one morning upon waking, suddenly to be much better at knowing the world?

5.8 Self-deception

Not only the "outside" world can render me mistaken; so can I. There might be deception of me, by me. Yes, that's right: self-deception is another possible source of inaccuracy. This is even more likely (I suspect, uncomfortably) when opinions in which I'm being deceived are about me.

This could happen whenever I'm thinking favourably about myself. On such an occasion, maybe I have reached too willingly for a flattering self-image. This is hardly a reliable way of thinking about oneself, if one wants to form accurate opinions of one's actions, capacities, and so on. Yet whenever I'm thinking well of myself, presumably I cannot know for sure that I'm not deceiving myself with inaccurate self-flattery. I doubt that I can ever *prove* this not to be happening.

The worry worsens: even self-*critical* thoughts can be self-deceptive. I've known people whose self-criticisms were merely part of regarding themselves as complex-and-therefore-interesting people. It was just a way of calling attention to themselves: "I have *so* many failings."

(These days, some lamentable TV shows welcome such people as tell-all guests!) Of course, I don't wish to be unsympathetic to everyone who is being especially self-critical. Some people are overly self-critical, seemingly self-hating, in a way that merits concern. In part, though, we pity them because they aren't being reliably accurate in how they see themselves. They should be *less* self-critical, if they want more accurate self-assessments—if they wish to know themselves. (They are seldom as lacking in merit as they think.)

Unfortunately, too, even self-assessments that are neither flattering nor overly critical aren't immune from doubt. If I form a neutral or moderately critical self-assessment, this could (without my noticing it) be part of a self-congratulatory attempt to fool myself into thinking I *can* assess myself accurately in this respect. It would be like flattering myself by thinking I don't need to flatter myself!

> *Control question.* Is it possible to control the formation and maintenance of every thought one ever has? Would this be desirable?

5.9 Self-involvement? Self-detachment?

That problem about self-deception raises a more general worry. When trying to know oneself, is there a perfect attitude or way of thinking (a "perspective") to adopt—guaranteed to be reliably accurate without being distorted by something like self-deception? If there's no such perspective, mistakes are always possible, I suppose.

Well, then, what perspectives *are* possible? If I try thinking about myself "detachedly," I'm striving to assess myself "from afar," treating myself as "just another" person. Okay, but there is an associated possibility of being no more reliable in thinking about myself *than* in my assessments of others. If I know the same about everyone, most likely I don't know much about anyone. I would know only "basic" or "generic" aspects of everyone—including, therefore, myself. This isn't to say I would never be accurate in beliefs about myself. However, I mightn't be especially *reliable* in those beliefs. I make many mistakes in assessing other people. Surely I could do the same when observing, and reflecting upon, myself from a similarly "removed" or "distant" perspective.

So, can I assess myself instead from a "middle" perspective, such as that of a good friend? Hmm. Presumably I would notice more of my details than if I was a stranger to myself; and I would retain some detachment, able to notice failings along with strengths.

Yet how am I ever to know for sure that my perspective on myself is so aptly balanced? For a start, *how* good a friend should I be to myself, when assessing myself? There might be no unequivocally correct way to answer this. If I'm too *friendly* towards myself, I could be more likely to assess myself favourably—just as it's easy to assess a friend too favourably. I don't think that I can ever know conclusively that I'm avoiding this danger in thinking about myself. Alternatively, if I'm too "*distant*" from myself, I might well overlook details, perhaps through inattention. Could I ever know conclusively that I'm not doing this? Probably not.

> *Emotional question.* Is there a perfect "emotional distance" to be from historical events, if one is to be reliably accurate in assessing, say, their moral significance?

5.10 Dreaming and the senses

I mentioned dreams yesterday, when asking, optimistically, whether they could provide self-knowledge. Now I'm thinking, more pessimistically, that dreams are a potential *problem* for my gaining self-knowledge. Here's why I'm thinking in that way.

Repeatedly in these meditations (particularly yesterday and today), I've found that my self-knowledge would depend on my senses supplying knowledge of a wider world in which I function. So, *are* my senses capable of doing that?

Well, to know the world by observing it is to have observational experiences. Day 3's account of knowledge requires these experiences to have arisen normally (and to be accurate in their portrayal of the world). In practice, I trust my observational experiences to be like that. Still, why couldn't my experiences sometimes arise abnormally and unreliably, without my noticing this happening? I would continue thinking, *but mistakenly*, that all is normal in my apparently observational experiences.

How could such abnormality occur? Here's one possibility: I am asleep *and dreaming*, even while feeling like I'm having normal and reliable experiences. Sometimes, my dreaming mimics what I regard as normal experience. My own history shows me how this effect can be present in dreaming's "after-effects." Occasionally, not long into my sleep, I've woken up without knowing I've been asleep; and I've proceeded to interact with people, even walking to other rooms to do this, while "in the grip" of what I'll only subsequently realize has been a dream. In the meantime, I'm saying things that reveal, to the other people, that I've been asleep and dreaming. I remain unaware, though, when doing this, that I've been asleep, dreaming. Although I am awake, in effect I'm being deceived by a "lingering" dream.

Thus, even when feeling like I'm awake, sensing in a normal and reliable way, I should admit that this feeling *could* be part of a dream, or at least a dream's "after-effect." In spite of thinking that I'm observing the world normally, I would be wrong. Even now, therefore, while looking around, might I be misled in that way? Grudgingly, I concede the possibility: there's a chance of my being in that weird situation, even though I don't feel that I am.

How would I try, then, to know that I'm observing, not dreaming? I would introspect, examining my present experiences for whether they have a dream-like quality. Yet that's not a conclusive method. What *is* a dream-like quality? As I admitted a moment ago, it's possible to dream in a way that mimics what I think are *normal* experiences. So, right now, I could be having a *stable* dream, an *orderly* one. It would be a dream, all the same; and it wouldn't be revealing the world in a way that amounts to my knowing that world.

In which case, it's not clear that I can *ever* know for sure that I'm observing the world normally. If even apparently normal observational experiences could be instances of dreaming (of "orderly" or "stable" dreaming), then I cannot ever know for sure that I'm not dreaming in that way instead. The only possible evidence I could consult (to gain this reassuring knowledge) would be the experiences themselves; but *they* cannot tell me conclusively what has caused them.

Really, they can't. I'm paying attention at this moment to what it feels as though my senses are telling me. I want to say I'm looking around me, seeing a messy and cluttered room. How can I check that this *is* what I'm doing? If I look closely, will I catch myself observing, not dreaming? No, because there are no observable, tell-all, signs of observing-and-not-dreaming. Nor can I, by concentrating hard, observe the mechanism underlying this current experience, so that I can see I'm seeing, not dreaming. I can't see *beyond* whatever I'm seeing; no power of "super-vision" takes over, once I focus well enough.

Yet if I cannot know for sure that I'm a being who is observing the world (rather than just dreaming it), my chances of self-knowledge in general are seriously weakened. (The past few days have impressed upon me the importance of observation to self-knowledge.) It's possible that I'll be left with no knowledge of what kind of being I am within that world. I wouldn't know myself as part of the world, because I wouldn't know the world in the first place. Of course, I also wouldn't know myself not to be part of the world (such as by being a non-physical thing). So, I wouldn't know whether *or* not I'm genuinely observing the world, as against merely dreaming. Obviously I could retain all manner of opinions about the world and my place within it; but these wouldn't be knowledge. A perplexing result!

Descartes developed a famous sceptical argument (sometimes called his "argument from dreaming") along lines like these. It is sceptical because it concludes that no one can know the world observationally. Potentially, it feels like a worrying way of thinking.

> *Intentional question.* Is it possible to form real intentions while unwittingly dreaming? Is it possible, while wittingly dreaming, to form intentions as to how one will act when awake?

5.11 Knowing something fallibly

So, it's time to confront the doubts I've awakened, to decide whether I *should* be worried by them.

The main question they provoke, I suppose, is that of whether I must conclude, sceptically, that I have *no* self-knowledge; and the answer to that question depends on whether it's possible to know something without having disposed of all related doubts that can arise. After all, I haven't answered every puzzling question I've posed over these few days about my ability to have some self-knowledge.

When contemplating becoming married, for instance, should the existence of even a single unanswered question or doubt lead to one's staying unmarried? Presumably not. It depends on how substantial the question or doubt is. This needs attention, because there are always questions yet to receive answers (even if only some people notice them). Even a marriage that succeeds might not have. One cannot know everything of possible relevance in advance. Even while married, one might not know every aspect of one's partner. The whole relationship, though it should be precious, will be fraught with fallibility.

I believe that my current search for self-knowledge is subject to similar tensions. Because of the unanswered questions, there's incompleteness in my thinking about myself. There are gaps in how well I can defend my beliefs about myself. This doesn't necessarily make the beliefs false. Still, it is a vulnerability. I should acknowledge the possibility of mistake, even in beliefs I hold confidently.

I'll call this a kind of fallibility—in that I am believing without *proof.* The past few days, then, show that if I have self-knowledge, it's based not on proof or conclusiveness, but on a continuing investigation, or on one that in theory could be improved. Further thinking might answer questions I'm currently leaving to one side (maybe as too difficult to answer immediately). Perhaps there are subtleties I don't yet notice, bearing upon what could be known. So, whatever I would know, I would know less subtly, fully, and completely than is possible. *Is* this how I know myself?

Here's an example. On Day 1, I asked how I could know that this hand is mine. Normally, it wouldn't occur to me to question my knowing this. On that first day, though, I entertained many challenges, perplexities, and doubts. Today, more have arisen, such as the argument about dreaming. Do I therefore not know that this hand is mine? Well, I don't *know*—I'll say that even louder (no one else can hear me!): I don't KNOW—this hand to be mine. These uses of emphasis are crucial. They concede that, given my unanswered doubts, I don't know *conclusively* that this is my hand. I don't *know* (or KNOW), because I haven't found conclusive answers to my philosophical doubts: there are subtleties involved of which I cannot be completely confident. Until I answer these probing questions, therefore, I must allow that none of my evidence *proves* this to be my hand.

All right, but what follows from this? The following questions arise, for a start. Does my not *knowing* (emphasis again!) something prove that I don't know (no emphasis) it at all? Is all knowledge really *knowledge*? That is the question of whether all knowledge is *emphatic* knowledge, conclusive knowledge. If that's what knowledge always is, then I know this hand to be mine, only if I *know* or KNOW it is—only if I can *prove* it is.

Yet maybe we aren't forced to adopt such a demanding picture of knowledge. Day 3's account of knowledge (as a well-supported and accurate opinion) didn't imply that all knowledge rests upon proof. For instance, that account is open to the possibility of my knowing this to be my hand, by thinking it's my hand, by being correct, and by using everyday (and good) evidence to support my opinion. (The evidence needn't amount to a proof. Presumably, it would comprise good observational evidence, such as an appearance of a hand, and my feeling that I can control some of its movements. My evidence would strongly favour the truth, without being a proof, of my belief that a "my-hand" is here.)

Obviously, this isn't conclusive knowledge. I don't know beyond *all possible* doubt that this hand is mine. I'm not knowing it *for sure* (this being a phrase I've used a lot yesterday and today). Can I know it anyway—without *knowing* it? In other words, can I know it fallibly—without having a *proof* of it? This is a vital question.

Caring question. Do some people care more than others about truth? How much should people care about it? (Which aspects of people's characters are touched upon by all of this?)

5.12 Usual knowledge

I wonder, however, whether less-than-conclusive knowledge—fallible knowledge— would be *inferior* knowledge. In one sense, yes, because it lacks a feature—namely, being a proof—which we might want knowledge to have. In another sense, no. I mean: if it is, then we are similarly inferior beings, continually making do with, and relying upon, lesser knowledge. After all, knowing something fallibly would presumably be our *normal* way of knowing (when functioning in our usual ways).

Why is this so? Simple: although normality can be reassuring and rewarding, it's also risky. It includes false moves, misperceptions, oversights, and the like—even in the midst of much accuracy, as our senses and minds guide us onwards. Yesterday, I reflected upon various "everyday" situations—watching movies, consulting friends and doctors, and so on—as potential sources of self-knowledge. None of these is immune from misleading me. In any use of them, error is possible: each is fallible. Yet this lack of any guarantee of accuracy is *part* of normality. It even helps to *make* a situation normal. Normality is imperfect; perfection would be abnormal! (Would a perfect mind be a human mind? I doubt it.) Far from being threatened by fallibility, therefore, normal knowledge would—precisely because it's normal—be fallible whenever present.

Now, does self-knowledge escape this thinking? Many people, as far as I can tell, would assume so. Self-knowledge is inherently special (they'll say): it involves no fallibility; it is conclusive.

I don't accept their view. These past few days show me that self-knowledge is not special like that. It shares too much with other knowledge. People's expectations of self-knowledge are unwarrantedly grand. It isn't perfect or conclusive, any more than other knowledge is. (Think of how often we look to science for answers to questions about ourselves. It isn't conclusive. Yet we walk away, satisfied that we've gained knowledge: "Oh, so that's why I react as I do to these foods. This is why I have those character traits. Finally, I know!") Given the questions I've raised, plus my being unable to answer them conclusively, self-*knowledge*—conclusive, infallible, *emphatic* self-knowledge—is unattainable. Am I concerned about this? No. Fallible self-knowledge would satisfy me.

Yes? Yes! If beings like us are to have self-knowledge, perhaps it *needs* to be fallible. Only then could it be *normal* for us, a usual part of our general functioning; and I want to know myself most of the time, with this being normal for me. Day 3's account would apply: any instance of my self-knowledge would be a well-supported and accurate opinion or belief about myself. However, the support needn't be conclusive. I don't have to *prove* the truth of my opinions about myself. These need to be well established, not perfectly so.

Okay, that's an easy thought to accept; and it has implications for how I should think. It tells me to hold beliefs about myself with some caution, because self-knowledge inevitably has imperfections. Humility, an openness to being corrected (by others or the world), is recommended. I'm a normal being in a world I don't totally comprehend and control; such beings are fallible, in all they do. (Even the best experts make mistakes.) So, if knowing is something I do, then I do it fallibly. (I just hope that I *do* manage to do it. Partly, it's out of my control.)

> *Normality question.* Roughly speaking, how many mistaken claims or opinions would be part of a normal day for a reasonably knowledgeable person? (A few? Many? Very many?) How often would a person have a day containing no mistaken opinions?

5.13   Infallibility

That approach won't satisfy everyone. Plenty of people insist that if there are lingering puzzles about something, it isn't known to be true. Puzzles should cause doubts; if there's doubt about something, is it therefore not known?

There is danger in that line of thought. Anyone who claims that there's no knowledge without infallibility might have to accept that there's no knowledge at all. After all, no beliefs or opinions are infallible.

Possibly, there is also "bad faith" in that line of thought. People routinely describe themselves and others as having lots of knowledge. Hence, it seems, those people don't really believe that knowledge must involve infallibility. If so, there's an underlying tension in how many of us think and speak. We regard knowledge as widespread, even while insisting that knowledge requires infallibility (which is rarely, if ever, attained). If infallibility is rarely, if ever, attained, yet knowledge requires infallibility, then knowledge is rarely, if ever, attained; in which case, it cannot be widespread after all.

How can this conflict be resolved? In practice, it could feel unsatisfactory to claim knowledge while admitting that there are related questions one cannot conclusively answer. It feels odd to say, for example, "I know I'm morally good, although I can't prove it. There are questions I cannot answer authoritatively about what makes me morally good." But would this prove that I lack the knowledge I claim? I'm unsure. What if I could proceed to offer a detailed, even if not exhaustive, defence of the claim that I'm morally good? Would this make it *reasonable* of me to claim the knowledge, even if I'm conceding my not having a *proof?*

Maybe. Here's one significant consideration. Suppose that, on some occasion, various questions I haven't answered, or objections I'm yet to undermine, are not especially good ones. Then I could be wasting my time by taking them seriously! In the meantime (perhaps while I'm still thinking that they deserve attention), should they be depriving me of the knowledge in question? I don't see why, even if they make me wonder whether I lack that knowledge. If an objection is bad, it doesn't deserve to be thought of as denying me such knowledge. (I'm just unlucky or inept if I haven't realized that it's like this!)

Still, until I work out how to dispose of the objection or answer the question, it's fair to say that I don't know *for sure* that I have the knowledge. I wouldn't *know*—that is, I wouldn't know *emphatically.* This could make me hesitate to claim the knowledge at all. However, if I'm prepared to take a chance, risking mistake, I might claim knowledge anyway. I should just recognise that I'm taking a chance—therefore being ready to relinquish the claim to knowledge, never being too dogmatic on its behalf.

Whenever am I *not* taking risks, though? Caution can be mistaken, too: *denying* myself some knowledge, simply because I think there's a possibility of lacking it, could mislead me. Can't my belief be knowledge even if I'm not completely sure it is? All things considered, I'm inclined to think so. (A possible analogy occurs to me. It could feel odd to say, "I'm a person, although there are philosophical questions I cannot answer as to whether I am—particularly questions regarding what it is to be a person." Even so, I'm not inclined to think that someone *is* a person only if he or she, or someone else, can answer all such questions conclusively.)

Infallibility question. Is it possible to mistake very good thinking for infallible thinking—and a lack of infallible thinking for a lack even of very good thinking?

5.14 Two pictures of fallibility

Where does this leave me? I'm not claiming to have proved that I have self-knowledge. If I'm right, that would be impossible: I cannot know conclusively, for sure, that I have any particular piece of knowledge. That would be to have emphatic knowledge—as I said, *knowledge*. This, I admit, I cannot have; should it worry me? Not if fallibility as such needn't be disastrous for a mind; and it seems to me that although there's a pessimistic, there's also an optimistic, way to portray what kind of failing fallibility is.

On the optimistic picture, fallibility is like a normal *limitation upon a muscle*. Being fallible in my thinking, yet able to gain knowledge, would be like my body's having limited but useful muscles. All muscles have limits; they can do only so much. Are they therefore hopeless, unable to accomplish anything? Manifestly, no. With repeated careful use, they become increasingly strong and useful. Maybe fallible knowledge, normal knowledge, is like this. (Even if my senses are forever fallible, they don't perpetually mislead. My memory makes mistakes—sometimes. When reasoning, I often do well enough—even if not perfectly.)

Then again, maybe not. There is also a pessimistic picture of fallibility. On this conception, fallibility is like a *debilitating illness*. Such an illness weakens the body a little, then some more, until ... possibly, death. Could fallibility kill the chances of any opinions ever being knowledge? The idea is that adding fallibility to fallibility, joining one risky belief with another, would build up so *much* fallibility within one's thinking that the initial failing is compounded disastrously—just as a dangerous weakness, when not removed, feeds upon itself, eventually making the body too weak to function effectively. No mind will ever have knowledge, so long as every move it makes leaves it increasingly vulnerable to falsity.

Which of these two pictures is more accurate? On the first conception, fallibility can be lived with, even healthily and productively; not so on the second one. The "muscles with limitations" model allows us to have fallible yet real knowledge. The "debilitating illness" model doesn't. Which is it to be? Maybe I'm strong, but imperfectly so, in my mental capabilities—strong enough to know much, even if not everything. Alternatively, perhaps those capabilities are diseased, weak from the outset and weakening ever more by the day—too much so ever to know anything, let alone much.

That is a fundamental choice as to how to conceive of fallibility in people's thinking. Maybe a little more reflection will help me to make the choice wisely. Let's see; that's what I will try next.

> *Metaphorical question.* Are metaphors ever our best chance of knowing something's nature? Are there situations where we could know something *only* through an analogy?

5.15   Living fallibly

It's odd, how readily people find fallibility frightening. If it's scary, so is everything we do! Living itself is fallible, able to end at any moment. Every moment I'm alive, I am fallible in whatever I do. Reaching out, my grip could close too early or too late. Taking a step, my foot might slip or a muscle could cramp. My thinking can go awry, in a multitude of ways. I am full of fallibility. Even when succeeding, I mightn't have done so. The potential for failure is ever-present, even in the midst of achievement. I only ever succeed fallibly.

Yet many people, it seems, expect knowledge to be an exception to the pattern of fallibility in all else they do. My hunch is this. They're forgetting that their knowing something is composed of much else about themselves—including clearly fallible aspects. Thus, my knowing is my mind's interacting with itself and with the wider world (by observing, remembering, and reasoning). I assess data, form opinions, notice this and that, compare, infer, and the like. Obviously, activities like these are fallible. None is ever performed perfectly. Still, knowing occurs when one or more of these skills is present or manifested; if we don't expect them to be perfect, we shouldn't subject knowing to that demand. To deny that knowledge can be fallible is, in effect, to deny that these skills give us knowledge even when being used normally and appropriately. What other pathways can we follow towards having knowledge, though? None. So, again we're denying that people have knowledge.

To me, that sounds too drastic. A more natural interpretation would reach for—actually, it might extend—the muscles-with-limitations model. We may interpret any situation in which a person knows something as one where he or she is skilfully using a *combination* of muscles that have limitations. Specific mental skills would be like individual muscles. Knowing something fallibly would be akin to a boxer's achieving a win, even by knockout, via a combination of punches. Combining the uses of the muscles was fallible—not guaranteed to succeed. It was effective nonetheless: the punches are thrown with skill, maybe with attention to detail. Is that how it is when I know something? There's a skilful coordinating of fallible but effective mental skills. Here, too, the result is ... power! A win! Possibly a knockout, if the knowledge is sufficiently strong and significant. Knowing would be like this—limited in reach and power, forever fallible, but potentially quite effective.

This is welcome news, if it's true. It certainly gives the muscles-with-limitations model more oomph! That model starts looking more realistic than the debilitating-illness one. Perhaps it isn't so hard, after all, to understand fallibility as not always emptying our minds of knowledge.

> *Skills question.* Do any actual minds have all possible mental skills? How much can people improve their mental skills? Does all such improvement consist in gaining new knowledge?

5.16 "That's life"

I'm musing upon all this while looking out of a late afternoon window—gazing upon a complex world, as cars move by, now swiftly, more often slowly. Reflecting distractedly, then carefully: "All right, I'm a fallible being, in everything I do. Even now, therefore, I'm being fallible." Intellectually, I accept this. Yet do I *feel* the fallibility within me at this moment? Particularly, do I feel it as a failing, a weakness or frailty—worthy of genuine worry?

I don't clearly feel it at all. My mind feels *successful* at this apparently normal moment: seemingly, I'm noticing my surroundings—cars, a road, parkland, people walking—accurately and normally. Even so, while pondering these past few days of philosophical agitation, *intellectually* I cannot avoid the conclusion that, even now, I am being fallible, no matter that I'm not *feeling* the fallibility. So, the fallibility is more like an underlying feature, felt only when "erupting" into actual mistakes—even if careful thought reveals its also being present at other times. Thus, I'm tempted to say that, while watching the world through the window, I am being only fairly successful. My intellect tells me to be a little muted in how complimentary I am to myself here. (I'm still not *feeling* myself to be doing "only fairly" well. Maybe this shows, however, that such feelings shouldn't be my ultimate way of judging myself.)

In other words, I must accept my being fallible right now, as part of living and knowing normally—even if I'm not feeling this fallibility. My present mental operations—this remembering, looking, listening, reflecting—are being done fallibly, even as I think these thoughts. While seeing the traffic outside, for instance, I could be misled. I admit this.

Am I thereby giving up on knowing? My intellect notices the fallibility; yet it also saves me. It tells me I *needn't* interpret myself as lacking knowledge: fallibility can be *part* of knowledge, not always a triumphant foe. I've found that if I'm not actually misled, and if there's nothing oddly unreliable in how I'm observing and thinking, then I needn't fail to know. Sure, I'll lack *knowledge*, emphatic knowledge. Even so, normal knowledge—everyday knowledge, fallible knowledge—might survive. Day 3's *well-supported-accurate opinion* conception of knowledge—a conception that was carefully derived, via reflection—allows this.

So, the fallibility forever present in my thinking is like a mole (not the animal!) that has always been with me, lurking on my skin. Although at any moment there's a chance of its suddenly starting to "go to the bad," it isn't a substantive worry until it does so. I cannot prevent its turning malignant. Still, until the mole takes that turn, it doesn't interfere with my body's working well; and this can be how my underlying fallibility affects my ability to gain knowledge. Until I become *badly* fallible, much knowledge would remain available to me.

Perhaps I even have much of the knowledge which, during these past five days, I've been reluctant to claim. My reluctance has been a response *to* my unanswered questions. Yet now, at the end of these meditations, I believe I understand why these needn't deprive me of knowledge: they might only be making my knowledge fallible. So I'm relieved, even happy; and now I must return to where all of this began, assessing anew. *Which* doubts (among those I've raised earlier) are serious and strong ones? Maybe not all of them are. How much fallibility is too much, if I'm to know something? Perhaps my doubts won't have uncovered *too* much fallibility in my attempts to know myself. I'll have to revisit my earlier philosophical questions and doubts—but without being frightened by fallibility as such, by what might be mere hints of possible mistake.

With which thoughts, my shoulders relax; and the world continues drifting past. There's an inescapable fallibility in how I live. All right, I accept this; only arrogance or fear should reject it. After all, although at any moment I could be about to fall into error, it also mightn't happen; and although at any moment I could already have erred, maybe in fact I haven't. Even if these mistakes never occur, fallibility remains, of course—perennially a vulnerability to error. (Nonetheless, it *needn't* ever be actual error.) I am subject to this potential problem in all else within my life; why not here, likewise? Knowing, if it exists, is simply a normal part of living. Like whatever else I do normally, my knowing is therefore fallible. Like the rest of me, it's normal, imperfect, and fallible. That's how

I am. I think I know this about myself—fallibly. Maybe this will be the beginning of *more* self-knowledge, then—albeit fallible self-knowledge.

> *Living question.* Does everyone have a philosophy by which they live? How extensive and accurate should it be?

5.17 Philosophical progress

These meditations began, on Day 1, with the question of whether I have self-knowledge. Since then, I've been immersed in intense self-reflection. Has there been progress? Yes. I've gained a more philosophically acute sense of how to think about myself (and possibly I've thereby *changed* what I am, too).

1. I've substantially clarified my initial question (of whether I have self-knowledge). Now I know better what it even means. It's replete with subtleties and details. Previously, I had little idea of how much there is to having self-knowledge. Now I do.
2. I've tested many hypotheses about myself. I've been trying to find possible answers to the question of what, if anything, I can know about myself.
3. Have I succeeded? Well, no answers have been unquestionably true. This isn't to say that none are true, though. It's just that there are depths and difficulties to negotiate in accepting any of those hypotheses. I would know nothing trivially about myself.
4. But that fact itself indicates something important that I might know, non-trivially, about myself. Cautiously, I've accepted a conception of myself as a fallible being, capable of fallible self-knowledge at best. This conception bears upon the basis of my being. Do I know it to be true? Perhaps—fallibly! I would know only fallibly of my inescapable fallibility.

5. More self-knowledge might then be available—always fallible, but self-knowledge nonetheless. I would stop looking for infallibility, as a required component in knowing. I would seek knowledge more relaxedly, expecting less of myself if I'm to have some. Science, friends, society, and so on, could then have much to teach me about myself, about my body, my character, and so on; as might my attentive observations of myself and the world. I need only remember that any piece of knowledge I could gain in such ways would be fallibly won or maintained; and I mustn't be frightened of fallibility as such.

6. I'll hold in mind the muscles-with-limitations model of fallibility. In general, I use my limited muscles sensibly, occasionally vigorously. If I expect too much from them, though, I'm likely to pull or tear them—which could make them useless for a while. So (by analogy), I mustn't over-react to the possibility of being limited, of sometimes making mistakes, in my grasp of myself or the rest of the world: I mustn't deny myself knowledge simply on that ground. Even as a knower, it's okay to think fallibly—just not very fallibly. I'll remain evermore conscious of my fallibility, therefore, monitoring it carefully but calmly—ready to discard any belief I decide isn't knowledge after all. Knowing is vigilance; and with this realization, for just a moment, I feel content.

I began my meditations, on Day 1, thinking that maybe there are *no limits* on what I can be; as perplexities flourished, I wondered whether I could know myself at all. I'm ending these meditations now, accepting that there *are* limits on what I can be, at least as a knower. There are limits on what and how I might know about myself. I'm also ending optimistically, though, wondering whether it's not so difficult, after all, for me to know myself in that more limited way. I merely have to concede, with humility, that my self-knowledge would be fragmented and fallible. Okay. Done!

Philosophical question. When, if ever, can asking a philosophical question change one's life significantly?

5.18 Overview of the day

Today has been climactic, taking me in two contrary directions:

Doubts. I've had a few—many, actually. Are there so many that I'm left with no self-knowledge? Is there no safe exit from this mass of pressing doubts?

Optimism. There is an escape from that danger, if fallible knowledge is possible. I've tried to explain why fallibility as such (which accompanies unanswered questions) can coexist with knowing.

Maybe, therefore, I *can* have self-knowledge. I simply need to accept that it will be fallible, never eliminating all possibility of error. On the other hand, perhaps my having fallible self-knowledge is also my *normal* or *usual* state. That would be a welcome result.

Unsurprisingly, questions persist. Here are some tantalizing ones:

Can there be better or worse self-knowledge? Might people improve their knowledge of having a free will, say, through philosophical reflection? If, with greater maturity, people know more of their characteristics, will this improve their knowledge of these aspects of themselves? For example, could knowing more about how one has acted improve the knowledge that one is cowardly or, for that matter, brave in some respect?

I hope that one *can* improve one's self-knowledge; and I'll try. Right now, though, a refreshing stroll beckons.

When I walk
I part the air
and always
the air moves in
to fill the spaces
where my body's been.

We all have reasons
for moving.
I move
to keep things whole.

> Mark Strand, from "Keeping
> Things Whole"

FURTHER READING

I began today by thinking about potential sources of mistaken opinions. Goldman's *Epistemology and Cognition* (Cambridge, MA: Harvard University Press, 1986) is helpful here: on perception (§5.2), see his chapter 9; on memory (§5.3), see his chapter 10. On computational limitations (§5.4), see Christopher Cherniak, *Minimal Rationality* (Cambridge, MA: MIT Press, 1986). Chapter 13 of Goldman's *Epistemology and Cognition* bears upon both memory (§5.3) and complexity (§5.4).

Those doubts reflect observations of, and research into, ways we fail to believe what is true. There are also distinctively *philosophical* doubts to confront, as follows.

§5.5's problem, about whether we even have introspective knowledge, derives from Wittgenstein's famous remarks on rule-following and private language: *Philosophical Investigations* (Oxford: Blackwell, 1953), §§243-315, 348-412. For interpretive analysis of Wittgenstein's remarks, see, for instance, Colin McGinn, *Wittgenstein on Meaning*

(Oxford: Blackwell, 1984), chapters 1 and 3. (§5.5 mentioned Chomsky. On his ideas about the innateness of some knowledge of grammar, see Michael Devitt and Kim Sterelny, *Language and Reality* (Cambridge, MA: MIT Press, 1987), chapter 6.)

§5.6's doubts—often called Humean inductive scepticism—are even more venerable and famous. See Hume's *Enquiry Concerning Human Understanding*, §IV. For an interpretation of his reasoning, see, for instance, Stephen Buckle, *Hume's Enlightenment Tract* (Oxford: Oxford University Press, 2001), Part 2, Section IV.

Those various doubts were jointly applied in §5.7, to the significant test case of love. For a non-sceptical proposal as to how one might know that one is in love, see Nussbaum's "Love's Knowledge," in *Love's Knowledge* (New York: Oxford University Press, 1990).

Then, in §5.10, another of philosophy's most significant sceptical challenges arose—Descartes's dreaming argument. See his "Meditation I." For commentary on Descartes's reasoning, see, for example, Margaret Wilson, *Descartes* (London: Routledge & Kegan Paul, 1978), chapter I. On the philosophical import of Descartes's sort of reasoning, see Charles Dunlop (ed.), *Philosophical Essays on Dreaming* (Ithaca, NY: Cornell University Press, 1977); and Stephen Hetherington, "Fallibilism and Knowing that One is Not Dreaming," *Canadian Journal of Philosophy* 32 (2002), 83-102.

A non-sceptical response to those sceptical arguments then appeared (§§5.11-5.15). A *fallibilist* reinterpretation of such doubts was outlined. One influential form of fallibilism is Karl Popper's: see the "Introduction" in his *Conjectures and Refutations* (London: Routledge & Kegan Paul, 1963). For overviews of fallibilist thinking, see Stephen Hetherington, "Fallibilism," *The Internet Encyclopedia of Philosophy* (2005), at http://www.iep.utm.edu/f/fallibil.htm; and Adam Morton, *A Guide Through the Theory of Knowledge*, 3rd. ed. (Oxford: Blackwell, 2003), chapter 5.

The book began with my trying to know a hand as mine, an example inspired by Moore and Wittgenstein (as Day 1's "Further reading" indicated). The book now concludes, on a theme also to be found in Moore and Wittgenstein. It is the idea of having *normal* knowledge of something. Should we distinguish (as §5.11 urged) between knowledge and *knowledge* (i.e., *emphatic* knowledge, or KNOWLEDGE)? Doing so might reflect there being both weaker and stronger ways to know something. On this possibility, see Alvin Goldman's *Knowledge in a Social World* (Oxford: Oxford University Press, 1999), pp. 23-25; and Stephen Hetherington's *Good Knowledge, Bad Knowledge* (Oxford: Oxford University Press, 2001), chapter 1. The latter also introduces the idea of having *improved* knowledge of some fact—an idea behind the chapter's lengthy parting question, about improved self-knowledge.

Normal knowledge would be part of normal living. Hume himself tried to reconcile his sceptical doubts with "ordinary" living. See his *Enquiry Concerning Human Understanding*, §V—and, more generally, §XII. For interpretation of his thinking, see Stephen Buckle's *Hume's Enlightenment Tract* (Oxford: Oxford University Press, 2001), Part 2, Sections V, XII. Descartes, too, offered advice on living in response to sceptical doubts: *Discourse on Method*, Part III.

Does all of that constitute the final word on scepticism? I doubt it. The following include further discussions of sceptical thinking in general:

Keith DeRose and Ted Warfield (eds.), *Skepticism* (New York: Oxford University Press, 1999). [Difficult]

Stephen Hetherington, *Knowledge Puzzles* (cited above), chapters 17-27. [Introductory]

——, *Reality? Knowledge? Philosophy!* (Edinburgh: Edinburgh University Press, 2003), chapter 12. [Introductory]

Christopher Hookway, *Scepticism* (London and New York: Routledge, 1990). [Moderately difficult]

Barry Stroud, *The Significance of Philosophical Scepticism* (Oxford: Oxford University Press, 1984). [Moderately difficult]

A POSSIBLE
PHILOSOPHY COURSE

The Further Reading sections at the end of the book's preceding five chapters list more sources than a single course, especially an introductory one, would need. (Many of those sources are also not so introductory.) Here, I'll outline one potential grouping of some of the more clearly famous, yet reasonably accessible, readings. (For the citation details, see each relevant chapter's "Further reading" section.) These— or even some smaller grouping from among them—can be combined with associated sections from this book, providing the core of a first course on philosophical problems. (This book would introduce simple versions of central ideas, setting a philosophical theme of questioning and discussion. Then the other readings would deepen the questioning and discussion—especially by presenting more sustained arguments for favoured theses than I have done in this book.) The course would be emphasizing *epistemology* (philosophies of knowledge) and *metaphysics* (philosophies of reality).

As I'll indicate below, too, many of the following readings can be found in John Cottingham's excellent anthology, *Western Philosophy* (Blackwell, 1996). (His collection also contains further relevant readings, especially in Parts I-IV and VI.) His book can thus be linked with this one to generate a stimulating and substantial, but introductory, first course in some fundamental philosophical questions.

DAY 1

Descartes, *Discourse*, Parts I, II. (On being demandingly philosophical.)
Dennett, "Where Am I?" (On a person's being physical.)
Locke, *Essay*. (On the physical world.) [See Cottingham, pp. 80-85.]
Berkeley, *Principles of Human Knowledge*. (On Locke on what it is to be physical.) [See Cottingham, pp. 91-97.]

DAY 2

Descartes, "Meditation II." (On being mental.) [See Cottingham, pp. 145-51.]
Hume, *Treatise*. (On a separate inner self.) [See Cottingham, pp. 197-202.]
Locke, *Essay*. (On being a self over time.) [See Cottingham, pp. 187-92.]
Parfit, *Reasons and Persons*, §§95-96. (On whether identity matters.) [See Cottingham, pp. 209-15.]
Sartre, *Existentialism and Humanism*. (On being free as a self.) [Or, for material from his *Being and Nothingness*, see Cottingham, pp. 228-34.]

DAY 3

Plato, *Republic*. (On knowledge not being an opinion at all.) [See Cottingham, pp. 12-19.]
Plato, *Meno*. (On knowledge being more than true opinion.)
Plato, *Theatetetus*. (On what else might be needed.)
Ayer, *Problem of Knowledge*. (A standard suggestion as to what more is needed.)
Quine and Ullian, *Web of Belief*. (On knowledge and other people.)

DAY 4

Plato, *Meno*. (On reason and memory.) [See Cottingham, pp. 3-12.]

Descartes, "Meditation II." (On introspection and reason.) [See Cottingham, pp. 145-51.]

Locke, *Essay*. (On perception and introspection.) [See Cottingham, pp. 26-32.]

Hume, *Enquiry*. (On perception, memory, and introspection.)

DAY 5

Wittgenstein, *Philosophical Investigations*. (Doubts about private language.)

Hume, *Enquiry*, §IV. (Doubts about induction.) [See Cottingham, pp. 321-26.]

Descartes, "Meditation I." (Doubts—involving dreams—about observation.) [See Cottingham, pp. 22-26.]

Popper, *Conjectures and Refutations*. (On fallibilism.)

Hume, *Enquiry*, §V (responding to his doubts about induction); and §XII (responding to sceptical doubts in general). [For the latter, see Cottingham, pp. 37-41.]

Descartes, *Discourse*, Part III. (On living, in response to philosophical doubts.)

Edited versions of some of these suggestions—the selections from Descartes, Locke, Berkeley, and Hume—can be found (free) on the internet, courtesy of the eminent philosopher Jonathan Bennett. See <www.earlymoderntexts.com>.